BANGLADESH ECONOMIC CORRIDOR DEVELOPMENT HIGHLIGHTS

JUNE 2023

ADB

ASIAN DEVELOPMENT BANK

© 2023 Asian Development Bank
6 ADB Avenue, Mandaluyong City, 1550 Metro Manila, Philippines
Tel +63 2 8632 4444; Fax +63 2 8636 2444
www.adb.org

Some rights reserved. Published in 2023.

ISBN 978-92-9270-169-7 (print); 978-92-9270-170-3 (electronic); 978-92-9270-171-0 (ebook)
Publication Stock No. TCS230193-2
DOI: http://dx.doi.org/10.22617/TCS230193-2

The views expressed in this publication are those of the authors and do not necessarily reflect the views and policies of the Asian Development Bank (ADB) or its Board of Governors or the governments they represent.

ADB does not guarantee the accuracy of the data included in this publication and accepts no responsibility for any consequence of their use. The mention of specific companies or products of manufacturers does not imply that they are endorsed or recommended by ADB in preference to others of a similar nature that are not mentioned.

By making any designation of or reference to a particular territory or geographic area, or by using the term "country" in this publication, ADB does not intend to make any judgments as to the legal or other status of any territory or area.

Please contact pubsmarketing@adb.org if you have questions or comments with respect to content, or if you wish to obtain copyright permission for your intended use that does not fall within these terms, or for permission to use the ADB logo.

Corrigenda to ADB publications may be found at http://www.adb.org/publications/corrigenda.

Note:
In this publication, "$" refers to United States dollars.

Cover design by Francis Manio.

On the cover: (*Top left*) The Padma Bridge connecting northeastern part of the country with the southwestern part. (*Top right*) Transmission power grid expanding power supply capacity and enhancing transmission network reliability in Dhaka and surrounding areas. (*Center*) A train waiting for passengers at the Gazipur city railway station. (*Bottom left*) Women returning home from the village market after shopping. (*Bottom right*) A worker at the machine tools operation section at the western marine shipyard in Chattogram (photos by ADB).

Contents

Tables, Figures, Box, and Maps

Foreword

Edimon Ginting
Country Director
Bangladesh Resident Mission
Asian Development Bank

Bangladesh has witnessed strong economic growth in the past decade. The economy has sustained growth at an average rate of more than 6% annually in the last 10 years despite the impacts of coronavirus disease (COVID-19) pandemic and surpassed the threshold of a lower middle-income country in 2015. The upsurge in Bangladesh's economy has been primarily driven by the rising share of manufacturing output to Bangladesh's gross domestic product coupled with strong growth in exports, partly helped by the country's least developed country status with various trade privileges and preferential treatment. Consolidating the gains of the last decade, Bangladesh aspires to become an upper middle-income country by 2031 and a high-income country by 2041.

While these targets are achievable, several binding constraints will confront policymakers as they need to implement a massive structural transformation program that promotes inclusive, equitable, and sustainable economic growth. Bangladesh is set to graduate from least developed country status in 2026. In the near future, as Bangladesh expects to enter the next phase of economic growth, both the advantages of low-cost labor and preferential market access may fade away and bring down competitiveness of traditional labor-based manufacturing industries. At present, Bangladesh has its economic growth concentrated mainly in the Dhaka and Chattogram divisions, while other districts such as Khulna, Mongla, Sylhet, Rangpur, Netrokona, Sunamganj, Panchagarh, Nilphamari, and others are lagging behind, and do not have adequate physical and social infrastructure to promote their growth in the future.

Therefore, to address these challenges, Bangladesh needs a holistic development strategy that will facilitate structural transformation and improve welfare across the country. An economic corridor is one such integrated development tool that enhances infrastructure, enables industrial proliferation, creates employment, connects production centers with urban and social agglomerations, and decentralizes development away from the country's developed areas. The Asian Development Bank (ADB) has prepared *Bangladesh Economic Corridor Development Highlights* to assess the economic potential of the northeast and southwest Bangladesh regions and propose holistic development of the regions to achieve inclusive and sustainable development. This study outlines a corridor development framework through industrial development supported by adequate infrastructure and a sound institutional structure. This study outlines broad categories of industries to be promoted, infrastructure and socioeconomic institutions to be developed, and institutional arrangements.

ADB has already provided support to several development projects along the Bangladesh Economic Corridor. These include South Asia Subregional Economic Cooperation Dhaka–Sylhet Corridor Road Investment Project and urban development projects in Khulna district. ADB, in consultation with the Government of Bangladesh, will explore operationalizing Bangladesh economic corridor development.

Finally, I would like to express my sincere appreciation to all involved in the process of consultation, preparation, and publication of the *Bangladesh Economic Corridor Development Highlights*, especially the officials of Bangladesh Investment Development Authority and the Economic Relations Division of the Ministry of Finance.

Acknowledgments

The Asian Development Bank (ADB) prepared *Bangladesh Economic Corridor Development Highlights*. This *Bangladesh Economic Corridor Development Highlights* was prepared under ADB's Technical Assistance 9602-BAN: Knowledge Solutions for Inclusive and Sustainable Development to assess the economic potential of the northeast and southwest Bangladesh regions and propose holistic development of the regions to achieve inclusive and sustainable development. This executive summary combines the Northeast Bangladesh Economic Corridor Comprehensive Development Plan (CDP) with Southwest Bangladesh Economic Corridor CDP prepared earlier.

This study was undertaken with generous financial support by the People's Republic of China Poverty Reduction and Regional Cooperation Fund.

In this elaborate and extensive exercise, ADB was supported by several key public and private institutions and individuals. ADB would like to thank the following institutions for their cooperation in providing the necessary support in this exercise:

- Bangladesh Export Processing Zones Authority
- Bangladesh Electricity Regulatory Commission
- Bangladesh Economic Zones Authority
- Bangladesh Hi-Tech Park Authority
- Bangladesh Investment Development Authority
- Bangladesh Inland Water Transport Authority
- Bangladesh Power Development Board
- Bangladesh Railways
- Bangladesh Small and Cottage Industries Corporation
- Civil Aviation Authority of Bangladesh
- Cabinet Committee for Economic Afairs
- Dhaka Electricity Supply Company Limited
- Director General of Drug Administration
- Dhaka Power Distribution Company Limited
- Federation of Bangladesh Chambers of Commerce and Industry
- Power Grid Company of Bangladesh
- Rural Electrification Board
- Roads and Highways Department
- Urban Development Directorate
- West Zone Power Distribution Company Limited

Abbreviations

BAU	business as usual
BEC	Bangladesh Economic Corridor
BEPZA	Bangladesh Export Processing Zones Authority
BEZA	Bangladesh Economic Zones Authority
BHTPA	Bangladesh Hi-Tech Park Authority
BIDA	Bangladesh Investment Development Authority
BIS	business-induced scenario
CDP	comprehensive development plan
ckt km	circuit kilometer
FDI	foreign direct investment
GDP	gross domestic product
GVC	global value chain
GW	gigawatt
ICD	inland container depot
IWT	inland waterway transport
km	kilometer
kV	kilovolt
LDC	least developed country
MVA	megavolt-ampere
MW	megawatt
NEBEC	Northeast Bangladesh Economic Corridor
RMGs	ready-made garments
SWBEC	Southwest Bangladesh Economic Corridor

Bangladesh Economic Corridor Development Highlights

Bangladesh has witnessed strong economic growth in the past decade. The economy has sustained strong growth at average rate of 6.5% annually in the last 10 years despite the impacts of the the coronavirus disease pandemic. Consequently, it has seen remarkable rise in gross domestic product (GDP) per capita from $1,659 in fiscal year 2016 to $2,462 in fiscal year 2021,[1] surpassing the threshold of lower middle-income country in 2015. The upsurge in Bangladesh's economy has been primarily driven by the rising share of manufacturing output to its GDP coupled with strong growth in exports. There have been two factors behind this: (i) the low cost of labor in the manufacturing sector, which has remained the key determining factor of the country's competitiveness in the global market; and (ii) its status as a least developed country (LDC),[2] which has generated various international trade privileges.

The country is now aiming to consolidate these gains and accelerate its growth. As set out in its Perspective Plan 2041, Bangladesh aspires to become an upper middle-income country by 2031 and a high-income country by 2041. Perspective Plan 2041 also intends to address the global commitment of the country to achieve the United Nations' Sustainable Development Goals.

While these targets are achievable, policymakers need to implement a massive structural transformation program that promotes inclusive, equitable, and sustainable economic growth. Bangladesh is set to graduate from LDC status in 2026. In the near future, as Bangladesh enters the next phase of economic growth, both the advantages of low-cost labor and preferential market access may fade and bring down the competitiveness of traditional labor-based manufacturing industries. Furthermore, the advent of Industry 4.0 will challenge Bangladesh's objective of generating 30 million jobs by 2030, as employment-intensive sectors like ready-made garments, leather, and footwear will be disrupted with robotics, automation, and machine learning. In addition, Bangladesh has its economic growth concentrated mainly in the Dhaka and Chattogram divisions, while other divisions lack adequate physical and social infrastructure to promote their growth.

Therefore, to address these challenges, Bangladesh needs a holistic development strategy that will facilitate structural transformation and improve welfare across various regions. The Bangladesh Economic Corridor (BEC) is one such integrated development tool that enhances infrastructure, enables industrial proliferation, creates employment, connects production centers with urban and social agglomerations, and decentralizes development.

---

[1] Government of Bangladesh, Bangladesh Bureau of Statistics. 2022. *Gross Domestic Product (GDP) of Bangladesh 2021–2022*. Dhaka.
[2] The United Nations Committee for Development Policy found that, in 2018, Bangladesh met the criteria for graduation from LDC for the first time and in 2021, for the second time. In November 2021, the United Nations General Assembly adopted a resolution that graduation of Bangladesh from LDC status will be effective from 2026.

An economic corridor has three complementary components: (i) a trade and transport corridor; (ii) production clusters producing goods for both consumption in domestic market and for international trade; and (iii) urban centers acting as the major market for goods from the production centers and for goods imported through international gateways; they also act as a source of labor, technology, support services, knowledge, and innovation. These three components are woven into a common development blueprint that is supported by appropriate policy support and corresponding regulatory and institutional reforms. The ultimate objective of economic corridor development is to promote prosperity and foster inclusiveness through integration of lesser developed regions.

Currently, northeast and southwest Bangladesh are key lagging regions in the country. Hence, for uniform, holistic, and sustainable development across the length and breadth of Bangladesh, BEC has been conceptualized running from the southwest region (Khulna division) to the northeast region (Sylhet and Mymensingh divisions) via Dhaka (Map 1). The entire economic corridor encompasses 14 districts, covering 34% of the total population. Most northeastern districts of BEC are included in one of the six hotspots (grouping of districts facing similar natural hazard risk)—haor and flash flood areas—of Bangladesh Delta Plan 2100. Southwestern districts of BEC are predominantly represented in the coastal zone hotspot of Bangladesh Delta Plan 2100.

Along with high population and geographical coverage, the corridor region holds strategic locational advantages. There are eight major trade gateways in BEC region: Mongla seaport, Payra seaport, Benapole land port, Bhomra land port (four in southwest); Akhaura land port, Tamabil land port, Bibirbazar land port, Nakugaon land port (four in northeast). While Mongla and Payra seaports provide sea route trade linkages with the world (currently contributing about 11% of seaborne international trade), land ports in the region act as major trade gateways with India, contributing 36% of Indo–Bangladesh trade.[3]

Hence, the corridor region has inherent advantage for international trade-dependent industries from the perspective of importing raw material and/or exporting finished products. Besides, Northeast Bangladesh has an added locational edge with respect to cross-border trade potential with Northeast India, a landlocked territory with a market demand of $38.5 billion.[4] Leveraging the logistical advantage, agri-commodities and industries from the Northeast Bangladesh region can find a potential consumer market in Northeast India. Likewise, Northeast Indian states, being endowed with natural resources, can export rubber, limestone and other mineral resources to Northeast Bangladesh, which can act as raw material for local industries. In addition, Northeast Bangladesh can leverage its proximity with countries like Nepal and Bhutan.

Not just locational advantage, the BEC region is rich in agriculture produce and it has an abundance of natural resources. The BEC region contributes 27% of fish production (the Khulna and Mymensingh districts contribute the most), 50% of tea production (the Sylhet and Habiganj districts contribute significantly) and 20% of rice production (the Khulna, Mymensingh, and Netrokona districts contribute the most) of the country. In addition, the Northeast region has an abundance of natural resources. It has significant the natural gas reserves (more than 4,000 billion cubic feet), which can be used for nonmetallic mineral industries and can also be used for production of power. Most of the

---

3   Government of Bangladesh, Ministry of Shipping; Government of Bangladesh, Bangladesh Bureau of Statistics; Government of India, Directorate General of Commercial Intelligence and Statistics.
4   Government of India, Ministry of Statistics and Program Implementation.

Map 1: Geographic Location of Bangladesh Economic Corridor Region

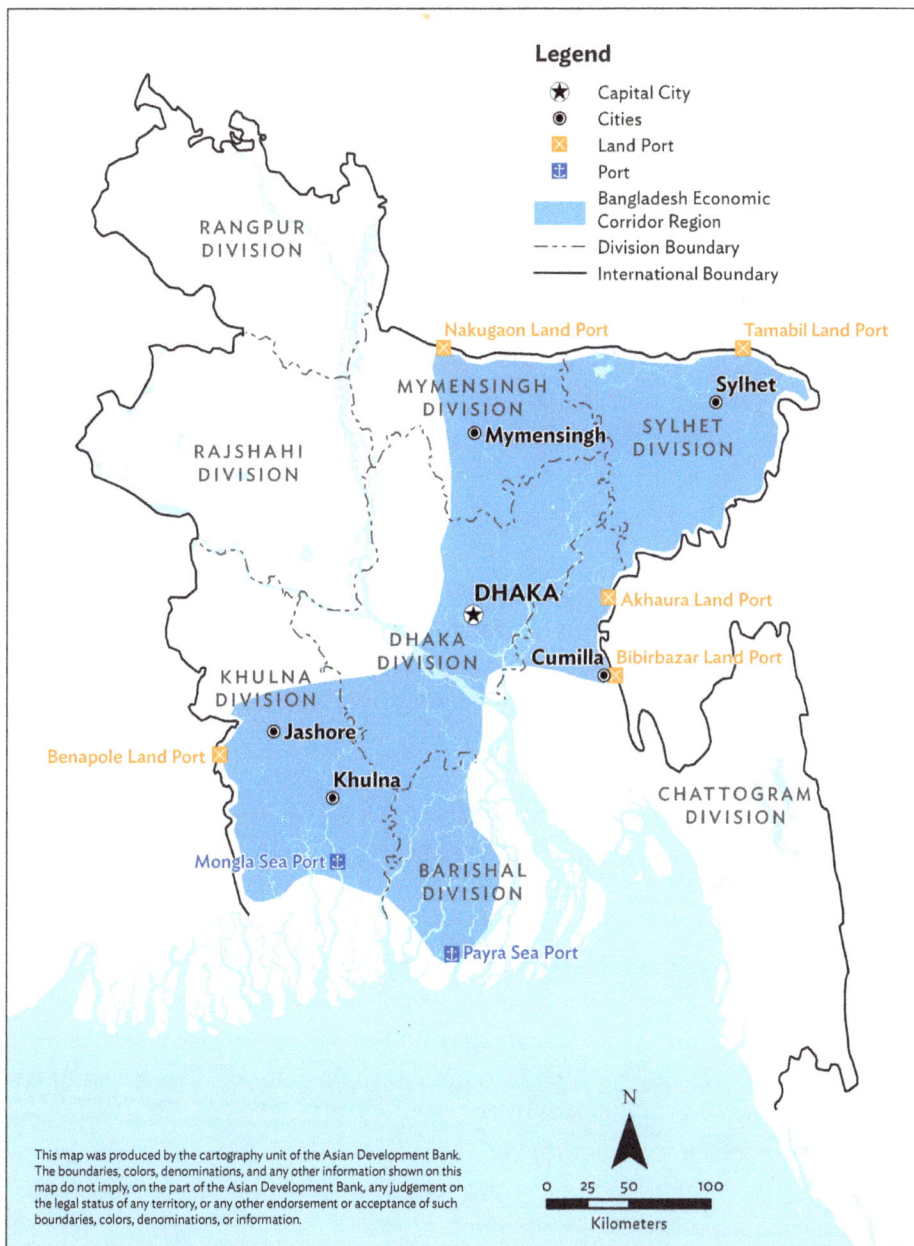

Source: Asian Development Bank study team.

gas reserves are located in the Habiganj, Kishoreganj, Sylhet, and Brahmanbaria districts. Apart from gas, limestone, white clay, and peat reserves are found in the Sylhet and Mymensingh divisions, which can be used in the cement and ceramic industry.

Despite being strategically located and resource-rich, to date, the southwest and northeast regions have not been able to fully utilize their natural advantages due to inadequate transport infrastructure within the hinterland and connectivity with the trade gateways. The absence of bridges at important river junctions (like Paturia) compels ferry crossings, which increases travel time and freight logistics cost.

Furthermore, presence of a *haor* area (flood-prone shallow land) in Sunamganj, Netrokona, and Habiganj districts restricts infrastructure development in these districts. Consequently, road density in many districts of the BEC region is below the national average. For example, the road density of Habiganj, Khulna, and Netrokona districts are 136 kilometers (km), 146 km, and 176 km per 100 square kilometers, respectively, as compared to the national average of 238 km per 100 square kilometers. Furthermore, gauge compatibility issues hinder railway connectivity. Also, shallow inland waterways dominate the corridor region, hindering inland waterway transport (IWT) beyond Dhaka.

Along with road, rail, and IWT, trade gateways of the corridor region also face capacity constraints. The only operational seaport of the corridor region, Mongla port, is constrained by low draft and inadequate cargo infrastructure. There are four operational airports in the corridor region: Dhaka, Jashore, Barishal, and Sylhet. Of these, Dhaka and Sylhet airports face capacity constraints (until current expansion projects get completed). Besides, all six land ports in the entire corridor region face challenges with respect to the lack of last-mile connectivity. In addition, Benapole land port, handling fully 28% of Indo–Bangladesh trade, faces an acute lack of storage capacity (existing capacity of 40,000 tons against requirement of 100,000 tons).

In addition, the BEC region is currently reeling under power infrastructure challenges. The demand quantum in the region adds up to 5,965 megawatts (MW) against the estimated supply capacity of 5,910 MW. This mismatch could widen further if adequate measures are not planned. Currently, the total installed generation capacity in the BEC region is 8,400 MW, which is 42.5% of the total installed capacity of the nation. On the distribution front, the region has a customer base of 12 million.

Apart from limited physical infrastructure, inadequate social infrastructure is also a key reason behind the poor economic development. The corridor region lags behind the country in terms of educational infrastructure. It has 317 schools per million population, as compared to the national average of 411 schools per million population.[5] The level of higher education in the corridor region (3.7%) is also lower than the country average (3.89%), indicating a higher number of people involved in primary employment, leading to underdeveloped human capital. The region also fares lower than the rest of the country in healthcare infrastructure. The average number of hospital beds per million population in the whole economic corridor region is only 496 compared to the national average of 668 (footnote 5).

Inadequate physical and social infrastructure in the corridor region, as mentioned above, has created relatively lower employment potential in industrial and service sectors (relatively high wage-paying sectors), which is corroborated by the employment number: 58% of the population in the corridor region is employed in agriculture, compared to the national average of 48%.[6]

Hence, with the objective of uniform and decentralized development, BEC is formulated to address industrial, transport, and social infrastructure. The development of this envisaged corridor may be carried out in two phases (Map 2). In the first phase, the southwest portion of the corridor may be developed (Southwest Bangladesh Economic Corridor [SWBEC]); in the second phase, the northeast portion of the corridor (from Dhaka to Sylhet and Mymensingh) may be developed (North-East Bangladesh Economic Corridor [NEBEC]).

5   Government of Bangladesh, Bangladesh Bureau of Statistics. 2019. *District Statistics*. Dhaka.
6   Government of Bangladesh, Bangladesh Bureau of Statistics. *Labour Force Survey 2016-17*. Dhaka

Map 2: Phase 1 and Phase 2 of Bangladesh Economic Corridor Region

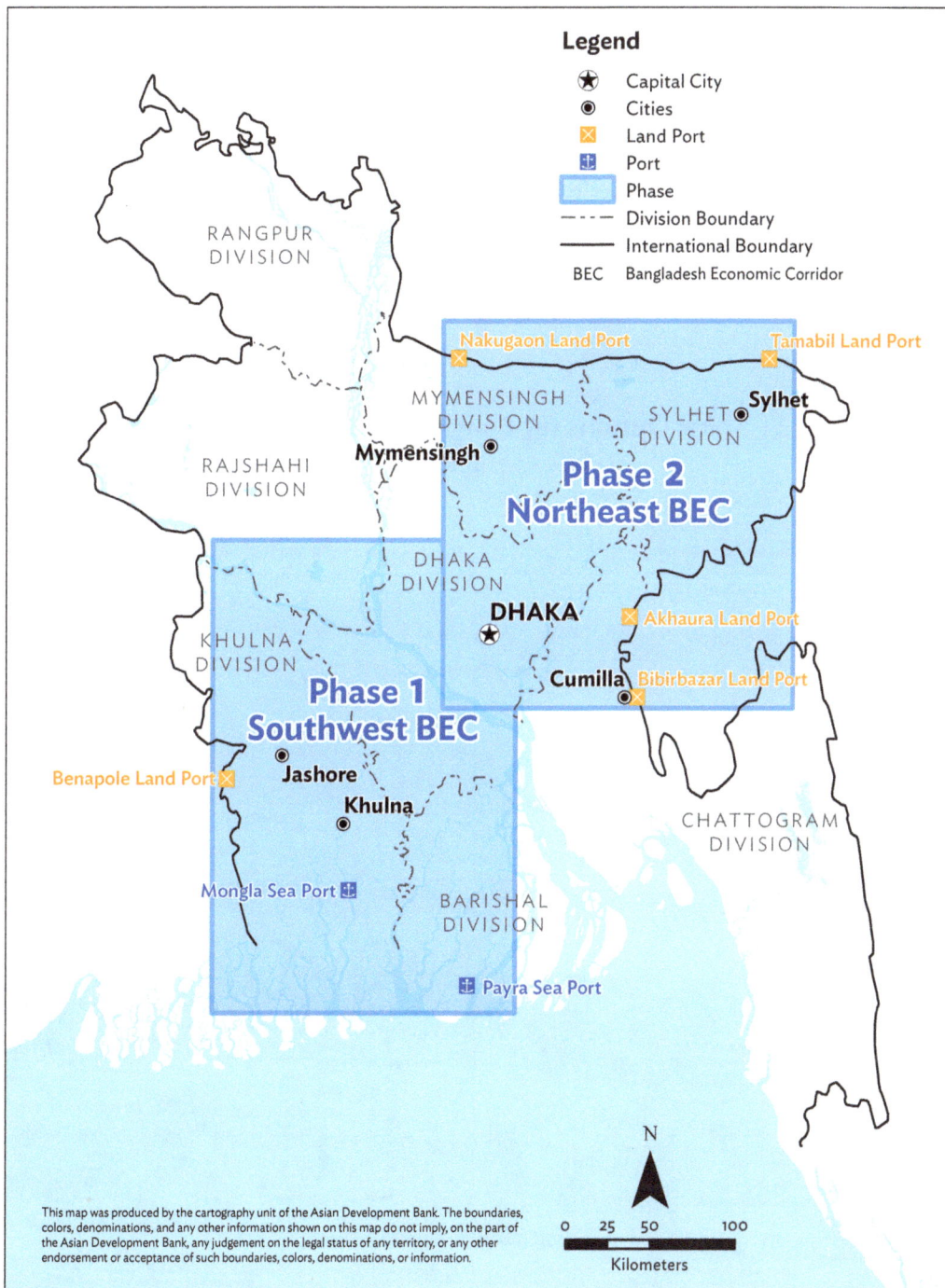

BEC = Bangladesh Economic Corridor.
Source: Asian Development Bank study team.

Any economic corridor entails constructing infrastructure, typically aligned with a major transport network, and connecting urban clusters with vibrant industrial zones for providing the necessary ecosystem for economic development. It also aims to maximize the population benefiting from socioeconomic development. This trunk transport corridor acts as the spine of an economic corridor.

There are three terminals of the envisaged SWBEC: Dhaka, Jashore, and Khulna. There are five spines (transport routes) that can connect these three terminals. Similarly, the two terminals of the envisaged NEBEC are Mymensingh and Sylhet. There are three spines (transport routes) that can connect Mymensingh to Sylhet (owing to the *haor* area in Sunamganj district, Mymensingh and Sylhet cannot be directly connected). All these options have been evaluated to select the most suitable options for SWBEC and NEBEC (Map 3).

Map 3: Spine Options for Bangladesh Economic Corridor
(Phase 1 and Phase 2)

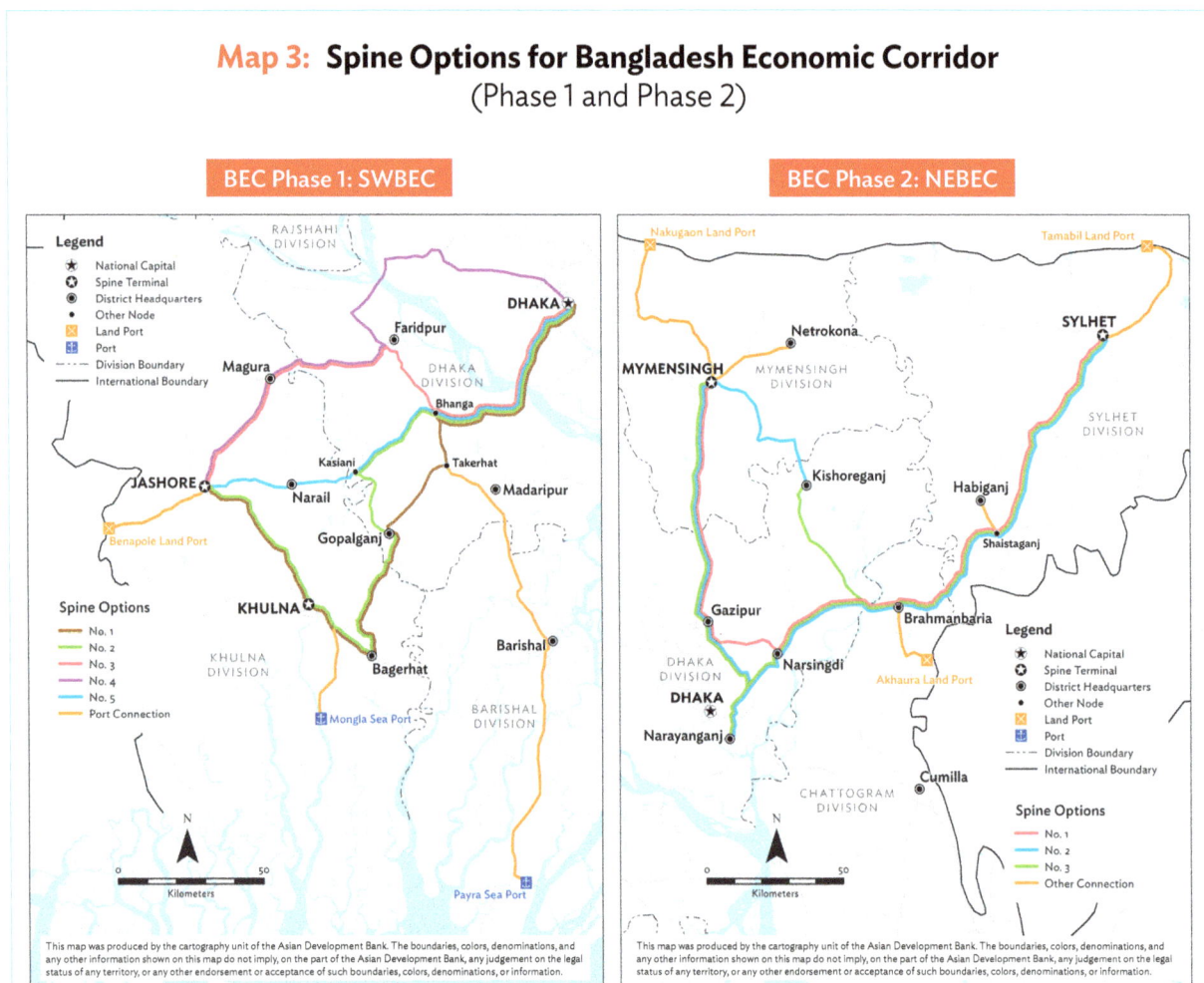

BEC = Bangladesh Economic Corridor, NEBEC = Northeast Bangladesh Economic Corridor, SWBEC = Southwest Bangladesh Economic Corridor.
Source: Asian Development Bank study team.

Box: Corridor Spine Selection

- **Spine Strength -** Length of spine, route condition, number of lanes, alignment to existing rail network, alignment to existing inland water transport network, alignment with existing power transmission lines.
- **Connectivity with Key Centers -** Connectivity to major production and consumption centers, trade gateways.
- **Population Coverage -** Coverage of maximum population through the network of corridor and its arteries.

Source: Asian Development Bank study team.

It is desirable that the spine of an economic corridor should have adequate capacity to carry existing and future traffic through multimodal transport modes, provide connectivity to maximum industrial and urban centers, and impact a significant population residing in the region. With this perspective, three options have been evaluated based on the following framework.

In terms of strength of the spine, option 5 has been assessed to be the best among the options for SWBEC and option 1 for NEBEC, on account of less congestion, a shorter distance, and high complementarity with other modes of transport (Table 1).

Table 1: Assessment of Spine Options on the Parameter of "Spine Strength"

Parameters	BEC Phase 1-SWBEC					BEC Phase 2-NEBEC		
	Option 1	Option 2	Option 3	Option 4	Option 5	Option 1	Option 2	Option 3
Length (km)	285	306.7	238	223.8	219.4	490	645	636
Volume capacity ratio	0.66	0.51	0.56	0.79	0.53	0.58	0.62	0.64
No. of ferry crossings involved	0	0	0	1	0	0	0	0
% of stretch with rail line running parallel within a lateral distance of 25 km	20%	40%	40%	40%	100%	69%	77%	77%
% of stretch with IWT route running parallel within a lateral distance of 25 km	0%	0%	0%	0%	0%	57%	51%	52%
% of total length under consideration for expansion to four-lanes	60%	67%	59%	29%	100%	60%	52%	61%
% of total length aligned with power lines	100%	77%	75%	29%	62%	85%	89%	89%

BEC = Bangladesh Economic Corridor, IWT = inland waterway transport, km = kilometer, NEBEC = Northeast Bangladesh Economic Corridor, SWBEC = Southwest Bangladesh Economic Corridor.
Sources: Asian Development Bank study team; Bangladesh Railways, Roads and Highways Department.

In terms of adequacy to provide connectivity to key economic centers, spine options 2 and 3 for SWBEC and spine options 2 and 3 for NEBEC have been assessed to be relatively better than the other options (Table 2).

Table 2: Assessment of Spine Options for the Parameter "Connectivity to Key Centers"

Parameters	BEC Phase 1-SWBEC					BEC Phase 2-NEBEC		
	Option 1	Option 2	Option 3	Option 4	Option 5	Option 1	Option 2	Option 3
Industrial areas connected (hectares)	1,824	1,824	786	788	949	3,287	3,324	3,324
Urban population served	86%	86%	71%	79%	79%	72%	100%	100%
Sea ports connected (no.)	2	2	1	1	1	0	0	0
Airports connected (no.)	4	4	3	3	3	2	2	2
Land ports connected (no.)	3	3	3	3	3	3	3	3
Major highways connected (no.)	12	11	12	10	12	12	15	15

BEC = Bangladesh Economic Corridor, NEBEC = Northeast Bangladesh Economic Corridor, SWBEC = Southwest Bangladesh Economic Corridor.
Source: Asian Development Bank study team.

Against the third parameter, population coverage, in the case of SWBEC, option 1 influences a large population. Options 2 and 3 fare better compared to option 1, as they cover 100% of the population within 50 km of the spine route as compared to 74% of population in case of option 1.

In terms of overall assessment, in the case of SWBEC, the combination of spine 1, spine 4, and spine 5 has been selected, whereas in the case of NEBEC, spine option 3 emerges as the winner with the maximum score based on the above three core parameters (Figures 1, Map 4, and Map 5).

Figure 1: Scores for Different Spine Options for Bangladesh Economic Corridor

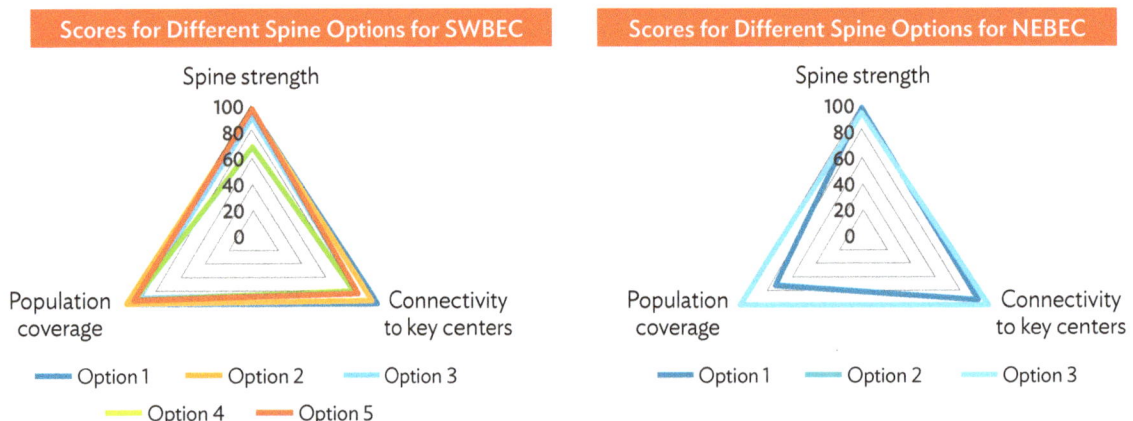

NEBEC = Northeast Bangladesh Economic Corridor, SWBEC = Southwest Bangladesh Economic Corridor.
Source: Asian Development Bank study team.

Map 4: Assessment Outcome—Selected Spine for Bangladesh Economic Corridor Phase 1 and Bangladesh Economic Corridor Phase 2

BEC Phase 1: SWBEC

BEC Phase 2: NEBEC

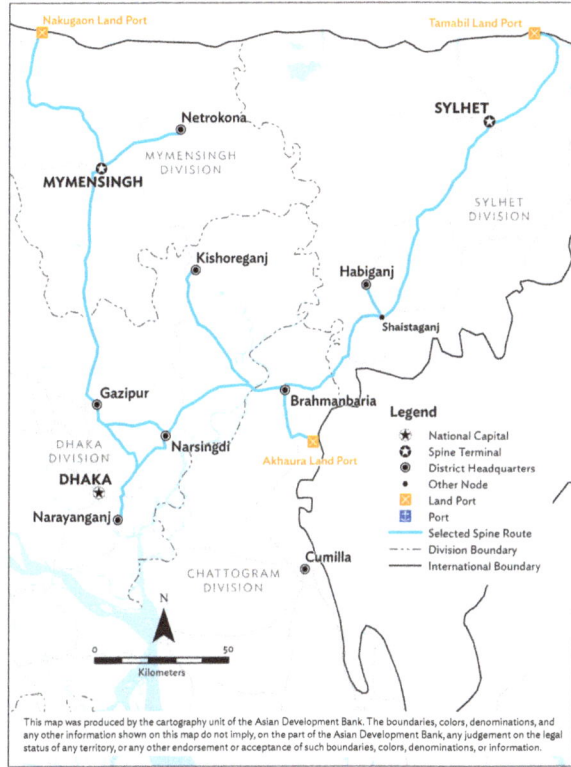

Legend
- ★ National Capital
- ✪ Spine Terminal
- ◉ District Headquarters
- • Other Node
- ▢ Land Port
- ▣ Port
- ━━ Selected Spine Route
- ‑‑‑ Division Boundary
- ─── International Boundary

SWBEC map labels: RAJSHAHI DIVISION, Faridpur, DHAKA ★, Magura, DHAKA DIVISION, Bhanga, Kasiani, Takerhat, JASHORE ✪, Narail, Madaripur, Benapole Land Port, Gopalganj, KHULNA ✪, KHULNA DIVISION, Bagerhat, Barishal, Mongla Sea Port, BARISHAL DIVISION, Payra Sea Port

NEBEC map labels: Nakugaon Land Port, Tamabil Land Port, Netrokona, SYLHET, MYMENSINGH, MYMENSINGH DIVISION, SYLHET DIVISION, Kishoreganj, Habiganj, Shaistaganj, Gazipur, Brahmanbaria, DHAKA DIVISION, Narsingdi, Akhaura Land Port, DHAKA ★, Narayanganj, Cumilla, CHATTOGRAM DIVISION

Legend
- ★ National Capital
- ✪ Spine Terminal
- ◉ District Headquarters
- • Other Node
- ▢ Land Port
- ▣ Port
- ━━ Selected Spine Route
- ‑‑‑ Division Boundary
- ─── International Boundary

This map was produced by the cartography unit of the Asian Development Bank. The boundaries, colors, denominations, and any other information shown on this map do not imply, on the part of the Asian Development Bank, any judgement on the legal status of any territory, or any other endorsement or acceptance of such boundaries, colors, denominations, or information.

This map was produced by the cartography unit of the Asian Development Bank. The boundaries, colors, denominations, and any other information shown on this map do not imply, on the part of the Asian Development Bank, any judgement on the legal status of any territory, or any other endorsement or acceptance of such boundaries, colors, denominations, or information.

BEC = Bangladesh Economic Corridor, NEBEC = Northeast Bangladesh Economic Corridor, SWBEC = Southwest Bangladesh Economic Corridor.
Source: Asian Development Bank study team.

Map 5: Selected Spine of Bangladesh Economic Corridor

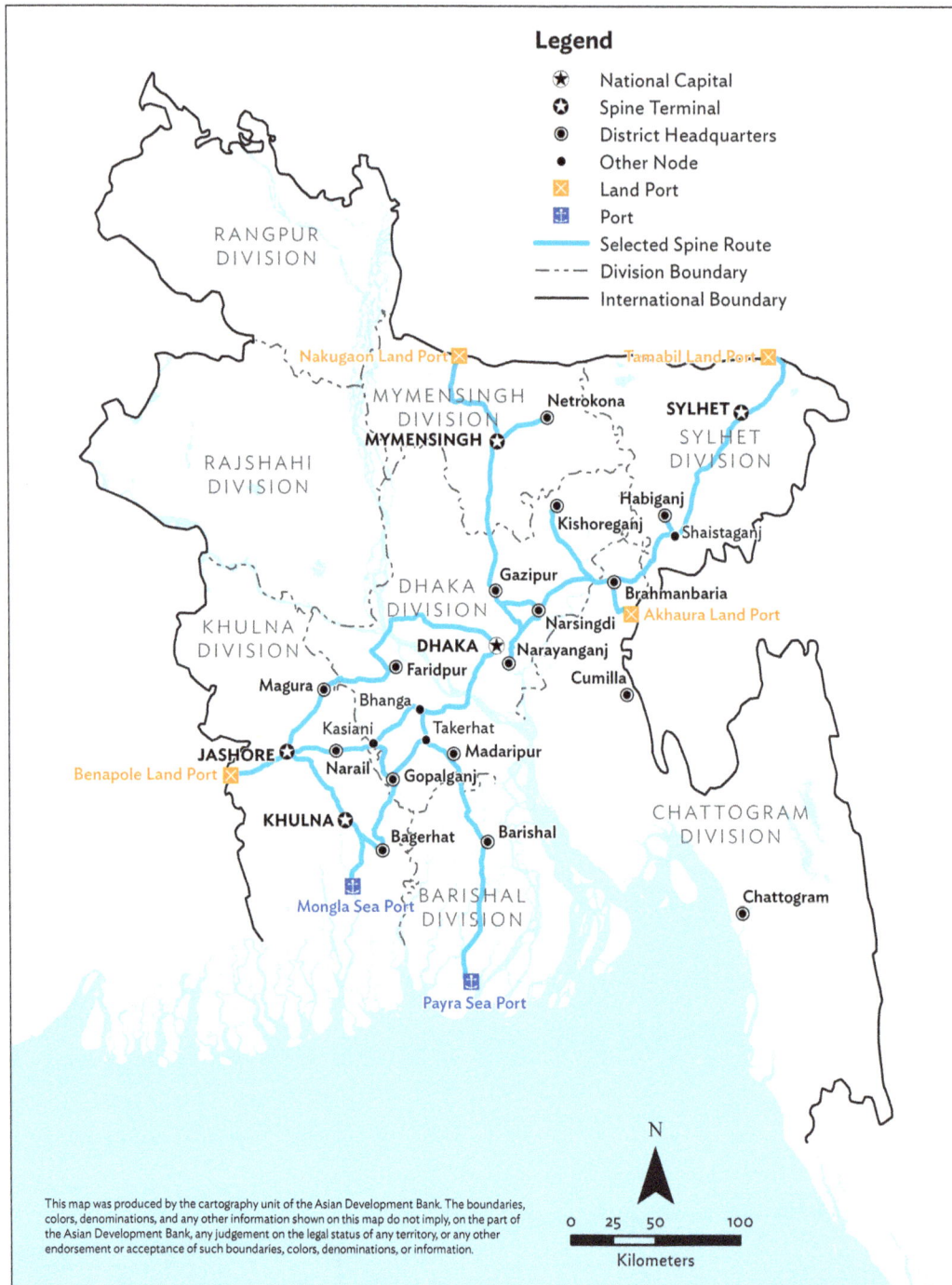

Legend

- ✪ National Capital
- ✪ Spine Terminal
- ◉ District Headquarters
- • Other Node
- ☒ Land Port
- ⚓ Port
- — Selected Spine Route
- —·— Division Boundary
- —— International Boundary

RANGPUR DIVISION

Nakugaon Land Port ☒

MYMENSINGH DIVISION

Netrokona

SYLHET ✪
SYLHET DIVISION

Tamabil Land Port ☒

MYMENSINGH ✪

RAJSHAHI DIVISION

Habiganj

Kishoreganj

Shaistaganj

Gazipur

Brahmanbaria

DHAKA DIVISION

KHULNA DIVISION

Narsingdi

Akhaura Land Port ☒

DHAKA ✪ Narayanganj

Faridpur

Magura ◉

Bhanga

Cumilla

Kasiani

Takerhat

JASHORE ✪

Narail

Madaripur

Benapole Land Port ☒

Gopalganj

CHATTOGRAM DIVISION

KHULNA ✪

Bagerhat

Barishal

Chattogram

Mongla Sea Port ⚓

BARISHAL DIVISION

Payra Sea Port ⚓

N

This map was produced by the cartography unit of the Asian Development Bank. The boundaries, colors, denominations, and any other information shown on this map do not imply, on the part of the Asian Development Bank, any judgement on the legal status of any territory, or any other endorsement or acceptance of such boundaries, colors, denominations, or information.

0   25   50   100

Kilometers

Source: Asian Development Bank study team.

Along with selection of spine, the economic corridor development also requires identifying nodes which are essentially industrial clusters spread across adjacent districts supported by the spine. Nodes are selected based on land parcels proposed for use for industrial development and are identified within the corridor influence area based on discussions and data sourced from relevant government organizations such as the Bangladesh Economic Zones Authority (BEZA), Bangladesh Export Processing Zones Authority (BEPZA), Bangladesh Hi-Tech Park Authority (BHTPA), Bangladesh Small and Cottage Industries Corporation, and Urban Development Directorate (Figure 2). Clusters with more than 1,000 acres of land have been shortlisted. Furthermore, based on the above mentioned other factors, four nodes are selected for the corridor region: Dhaka–Gazipur–Narshinghdi, Khulna–Jessore, Sylhet–Habiganj, and Mymensingh–Netrokona (Map 6).

Figure 2: Corridor Node Selection Framework

1
Coverage of maximum districts in the corridor region
- Distance is less than 50 kilometers from either side of the identified spine
- Integration of the region with the end points of the spine and rest of the country

2
- Extent of land availability in brownfield and/or greenfield areas (minimum 404.7 hectares of land in a node)
- Direct access to minimum one trade gateway with northeast India

Source: Asian Development Bank study team.

Along with industrial development in these four identified nodes, Sunamganj cluster can be developed as the supplier of key input materials for industries in the corridor region.

The Dhaka–Gazipur–Narshinghdi node consists of seven districts: Dhaka, Gazipur, Narshinghdi, Kishoreganj, Narayanganj, and Brahmanbaria. These seven districts constitute 10,100 acres of land for development. Of this, 6,500 acres of land are available across 18 economic zones. As this node lies in the proximity of Dhaka, it is well connected by the network of national highways such as N3 (Dhaka Mymensingh Highway), N2 (Dhaka Sylhet Highway) and N1 (Dhaka Chattogram Highway) to the rest of the country. There are 74 technical and vocational institutions with a total capacity of 36,000 students.[7]

The Khulna–Jessore node consists of three districts: Khulna, Bagerhat, and Jessore. These three districts constitute 2,313 acres of land for development. Of this, 1,600 acres of land are available across five economic zones. Jessore, Khulna, and Bagerhat are well connected by N7, but have only limited rail connectivity between the two centers. There are 55 technical and vocational institutions with a total capacity of 12,500 students (footnote 7).

---

7   Government of Bangladesh, Bangladesh Bureau of Statistics. 2019. *District Statistics.* Dhaka.

Map 6: Selected Nodes in Bangladesh Economic Corridor Region

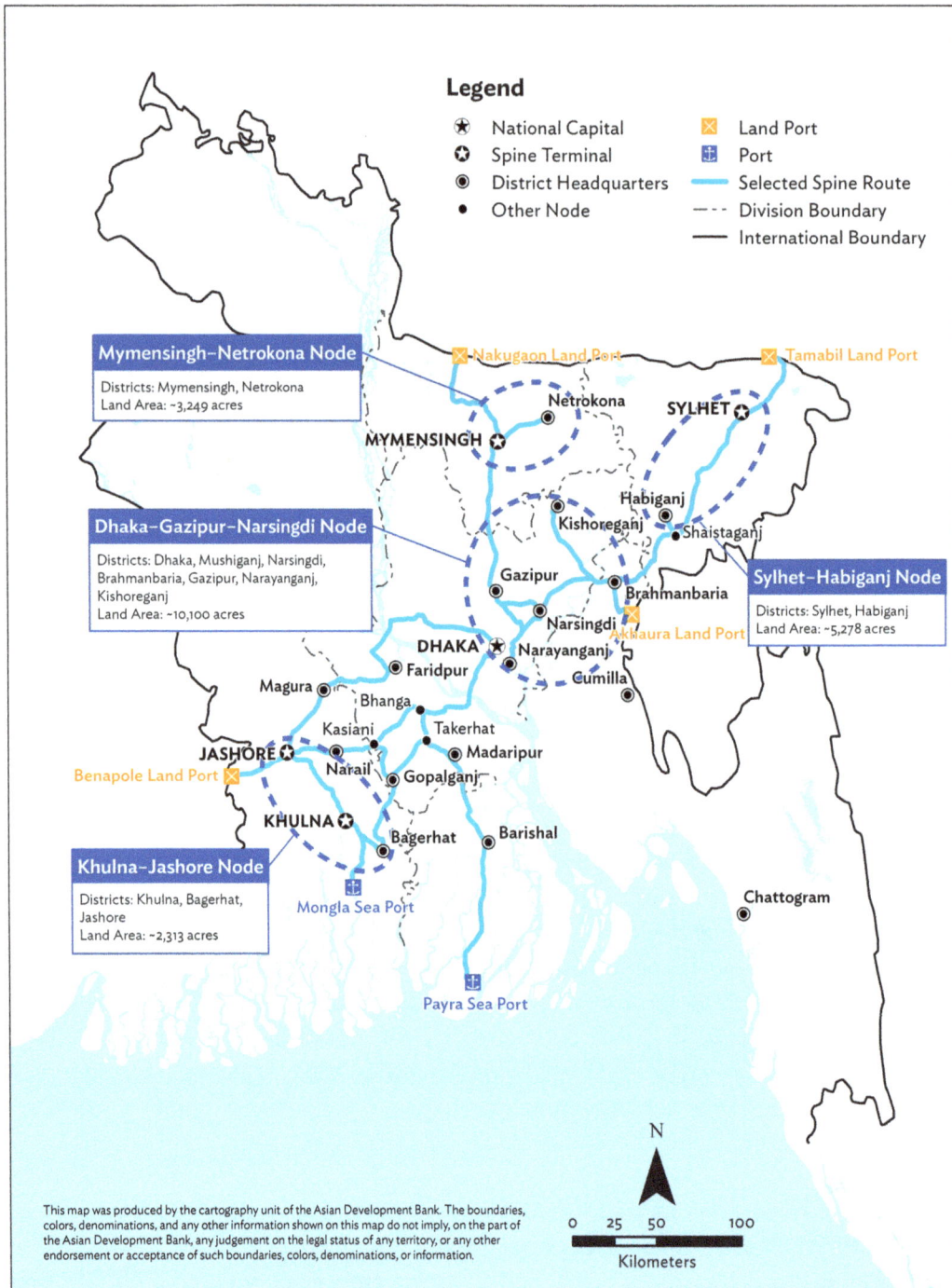

Legend

- ✹ National Capital
- ✪ Spine Terminal
- ◉ District Headquarters
- • Other Node
- ⊠ Land Port
- ⊕ Port
- — Selected Spine Route
- - - Division Boundary
- — International Boundary

Mymensingh–Netrokona Node
Districts: Mymensingh, Netrokona
Land Area: ~3,249 acres

Dhaka–Gazipur–Narsingdi Node
Districts: Dhaka, Mushiganj, Narsingdi,
Brahmanbaria, Gazipur, Narayanganj,
Kishoreganj
Land Area: ~10,100 acres

Sylhet–Habiganj Node
Districts: Sylhet, Habiganj
Land Area: ~5,278 acres

Khulna–Jashore Node
Districts: Khulna, Bagerhat,
Jashore
Land Area: ~2,313 acres

Nakugaon Land Port
Tamabil Land Port
Netrokona
SYLHET
MYMENSINGH
Habiganj
Kishoreganj
Shaistaganj
Gazipur
Brahmanbaria
Narsingdi
Akhaura Land Port
DHAKA
Faridpur
Narayanganj
Magura
Cumilla
Bhanga
Kasiani
Takerhat
Jashore
Madaripur
Benapole Land Port
Narail
Gopalganj
Khulna
Bagerhat
Barishal
Mongla Sea Port
Chattogram
Payra Sea Port

N

0 25 50 100
Kilometers

This map was produced by the cartography unit of the Asian Development Bank. The boundaries, colors, denominations, and any other information shown on this map do not imply, on the part of the Asian Development Bank, any judgement on the legal status of any territory, or any other endorsement or acceptance of such boundaries, colors, denominations, or information.

Source: Asian Development Bank study team.

The Mymensingh–Netrokona node consists of two districts: Mymensingh and Netrokona. A total of 3,249 acres of land is available for allocation for industrial, social, and utility infrastructure development. Of this, 1,500 acres of land are part of five economic zones in the region. Mymensingh district in the node is connected by N3 (Dhaka Mymensingh Highway) to Dhaka. In addition to this, Netrokona is connected to Mymensingh via a regional route, R370. A railway network exists in the node and provides connectivity from Mymensingh to Dhaka city and to Akhaura land port, ultimately providing connectivity to Chattogram Port and other parts of the country. There are 44 technical institutions with a total student capacity of 14,000 (footnote 7).

The Sylhet–Habiganj node consists of two major districts, i.e., Sylhet and Habiganj, with a total land of 5,278 acres available for industrial development. Of this, 968 acres of land fall within three economic zones, two of which are in the Habiganj district, and one in the Sylhet district. In addition to this, BHTPA is also developing an information technology park and electronics city in the Sylhet district, which is expected to occupy 800 acres. The node is well connected with Dhaka via N2 (Dhaka–Sylhet highway). The node hosts 14 technical and vocational institutions with a total capacity of 7,800 student (footnote 7).

These four nodes are prioritized based on land availability, proximity to existing industrial and urban agglomeration, proximity to trade gateways, availability of utilities, and availability of social infrastructure (Figure 3).

Figure 3: Framework for Prioritization of Corridor Nodes

Coverage of maximum districts in the corridor region

- Land availability
- Proximity to existing industrial and urban agglomeration
- Proximity to key highways, rail links, trade gateways, seaports, land ports, airports
- Availability of utilities and social infrastructure
- Availability and adequacy of labor force and presence of human resource development centers

Source: Asian Development Bank study team.

Table 3 summarizes the relative prioritization of the respective nodes based on the evaluation against the parameters as detailed above (Table 3).

Table 3: Evaluation of Node Prioritization

	Land Availability and Proximity	Infrastructure	Urban and Industrial Ecosystem	Skill Availability	Overall
Dhaka–Gazipur Narsinghdi Node	●	●	◕	◑	●
Mymensingh–Netrokona Node	●	◑	◔	◕	◕
Jessore-Khulna Node	◑	◑	◑	◑	◑
Sylhet–Habiganj Node	◔	●	◑	○	◑

Source: Asian Development Bank study team.

Determination of Right Mix of Industries, Holding Potential for Next Phase of Growth

Production clusters, or industrial zones, are one of the key components of an economic corridor given that these are where industrial production takes place. This component, when complemented by trunk transport corridors and urban agglomeration, becomes the main driver of growth of the economic corridor. To have effective and efficient production clusters, the right mix of industries exhibiting high potential for growth, both in global as well as domestic markets, needs to be promoted. In this regard, an initial shortlist of industries is prepared based on parameters such as: potential of export basket diversification (Haussmann Product Space Analysis), industries with highly geographically distributed value chain (Global Value Chain Index Analysis), export-import trade potential, potential for backward and forward linkages, high global market potential, domestic market potential, and thrust sectors identified by the Government of Bangladesh.

As the next step, detailed value chain assessment for each of these industries is undertaken to understand the intensity of Bangladesh's participation in each stage of global value chains (GVCs) and to assess the potential of expansion along the GVCs (forward and backward integration) of these industries. Based on the detailed value chain assessment, industries (and their respective value chains) are identified that will be easier to promote in the corridor region given its inherent advantages and disadvantages.

Based on the outcome of the analysis, 12 manufacturing industries were shortlisted for the whole BEC region: food processing, leather and footwear, textiles and ready-made garments (RMGs), jute, nonmetallic mineral manufacturers, shipbuilding, furniture, transport equipment, pharmaceuticals, plastic products, rubber and rubber products, electrical and electronics machinery, and heavy machineries.

As the next step, a detailed value chain assessment was conducted on these industries:

(i) **Food processing (agro and fish).** Tea and fish, two major agriculture produces of the corridor region, contribute 50% and 27% of the national production, respectively. Currently, Bangladesh is a net exporter of fish (with trade balance of $452 million in 2019), with India contributing only 5% in Bangladesh's exports. By setting up fish processing facilities in the BEC region, the region can utilize its proximity with India to tap the export potential. In the case of shrimp, the southwest region has 80% of Bangladesh's shrimp farms, offering a significant advantage for the industry. With tea, Bangladesh is a net importer (with import of $7.3 million and trade deficit of 4 million), which shows the region can supply to the large domestic market.

(ii) **Leather and footwear.** Bangladesh has a large trade surplus of $1.6 billion in the leather articles and footwear sector, and their exports have seen significant rise in the past few years. However, Bangladesh lacks the capacity to add value in the downstream stages of the value chain of leather articles and footwear. With the adoption of technology and modernization of plants, existing industries in the Dhaka–Gazipur–Narshinghdi node can become future-ready, with more value-added products. Also, the region has 42% of the country's cattle, which can provide easy access to raw material (raw hides).

(iii) **Textiles and ready-made garments.** Bangladesh has exported textiles and RMGs valued at $42 billion in 2019, contributing 84% of the country's export basket, dominating the industry. The industry has a major presence in the Dhaka, Narayanganj, Gazipur, and Narshingdi districts in the corridor region. Cottons and synthetic fiber are the primary inputs that are used in the industry. Bangladesh imports both of these inputs mostly from India (30% of total cotton imports and 17% of synthetic material imports) and the People's Republic of China (43% of total cotton imports and 57% of synthetic material imports). Considering that the industry is dependent on import of raw materials and is export-oriented, proximity to trade gateways is important. The presence of the Mongla and Payra seaports and Benapole land port would be beneficial for the industry in the corridor region. However, in the future, industries in the corridor region need to focus on more value-added products and enter lucrative value chain stages.

(iv) **Jute.** Bangladesh exports of jute products are mostly in the form of intermediate goods (fiber, yarn, and fabric) and not in finished products. This is corroborated by the fact that, in 2019, the total export of finished products was $113 million, while that of intermediates was more than $1.3 billion. Although jute has traditionally been a strong industry in Bangladesh, it has been consistently losing market share to synthetic fibers. In recent years, a trend of using diversified products of jute such as geotextiles, jute-reinforced plastics, jute laminates, decorative fabrics, carpets, and handicrafts has emerged. Furthermore, with rising environmental concerns, the use of natural fiber is likely to be promoted. These emerging trends provide a potential opportunity in the long run. Capitalizing on these emerging trends will require research and development, and focused marketing efforts. Existing establishments in the SWBEC region need to adapt to the new changes.

(v) **Nonmetallic mineral.** NEBEC is suitable for development of ceramic and glass and the glassware industry. The region offers easy access to raw material (clay and glass sand) in the Mymensingh, Netrokona, Habiganj, and Sylhet districts, and it also hosts natural gas reserves (more than 4 trillion cubic feet) required for the industry. Huge trade deficits in both the ceramic ($49 million) and glass industries ($165.7 million) represent a domestic market opportunity for the producers in the region.

(vi) **Shipbuilding.** Bangladesh is a net importer of shipbuilding industry products, with imports of $603 million and trade deficit of $590 million in 2019. Fully 70% of Bangladesh's imports were of light vessels, fire-floats, dredgers, cruise ships, excursion boats, ferry boats, and barges. However, a high trade deficit implies significant domestic demand, estimated to be $1 billion. Bangladesh's focus has mostly been on relatively smaller and simpler vessels. Considering this, it is likely that the technology available within the country currently may not be adequate to produce larger and sophisticated vessels. In addition, there is low participation of Bangladesh in the design stage. In terms of raw materials, while some of the inputs such as switch boards, steel cables, and transformers are procured locally, dependence on imports for machines and steel is likely to remain. Deliberate and focused government support is required to promote the industry and the corresponding backward linkages and ancillary industries. As stated in Bangladesh Delta Plan 2100, the government considers shipbuilding as a priority sector under its approaches to harness blue economy. Maintaining the growth of the shipbuilding industry and developing new maritime industries is a key priority.

(vii) **Furniture.** Bangladesh's forest cover is much lower compared to the global average. It is only 11% of the total land area of the country and is much lower than the neighboring regions such as Northeast India (65%) and Bhutan (72%). Due to unavailability of raw material, Bangladesh is highly dependent on imports of furniture, and its international trade in furniture features a trade deficit of $129 million. However, the high trade deficit implies significant domestic demand. Furniture establishments in the NEBEC region can import timber from Northeast Indian states and Bhutan. After processing, they can sell and capture domestic market demand. Bangladesh exports $54 million of mattress products (including coir). From the perspective of the supply of coir, the southwest region of Bangladesh stands at an advantage compared to other regions in the country, with the Khulna district being the top producer of coconut.

(viii) **Automotive and transport equipment.** Bangladesh is highly dependent on import of automobiles and transport equipment, with a total trade deficit of $2 billion in 2019, indicating a huge domestic market. The Trishal area in the Mymensingh node holds a few automobile facilities where the value chain is only limited to the assembly stage. However, in the bicycle segment, Bangladesh clocked total exports of $80 million in 2019. About 90% of these bicycles were exported to European Union nations. Leveraging its proximity to the Mongla and Payra ports, BEC industries can target the Asia and Pacific countries for export.

(ix) **Pharmaceuticals.** Domestic production meets 97% of the domestic market for pharmaceutical products in Bangladesh. But Bangladesh's trade deficit in pharmaceutical products is $163 million, with imports worth $280 million. The reason behind the country's high import is that most of the pharmaceuticals companies are involved in generic formulation manufacturing for which they import active pharmaceutical ingredients. Hence, proximity to an airport is needed for the industry. Considering that, the industry can be promoted in the Dhaka–Gazipur–Narshinghdi and Khulna–Jessore nodes. These nodes will also have an easy market access to Dhaka and neighboring districts. The presence of Dhaka in the corridor region and the expected development of urban areas in the southwest region should attract the necessary skilled human capital.

(x)   **Plastic and plastic products.** Bangladesh is highly dependent on the imports of plastic and plastic products ($2.5 billion in 2019). More than 73% of domestic consumption is met by imports, indicating its high import dependency which, in turn, implies large untapped domestic demand. Oil and gas are the major input product for the plastic industry and the country lacks adequate refining capacity; as a result, a significant number of final petroleum products are imported compared to crude oil. Northeast India has some oil refineries with excess refining capacity of 10 million metric tons per annum. This excess oil can be imported by poly-olefin plants in NEBEC. The domestically produced polymer can be used by the plastic and plastic article manufacturing industries located in the northeast and Dhaka division of Bangladesh.

(xi) **Rubber and rubber articles.** Like in the plastic industry, Bangladesh is highly dependent on rubber imports, importing $300 million of various articles in 2019. The absence of both chemical and petrochemical industries in the country is one of the major reasons why Bangladesh has no synthetic rubber manufacturing. However, rubber article manufacturing companies in NEBEC can procure the natural rubber from gardens in the Sylhet division and northeast India, and petrochemical products from refineries in northeast India. The produced rubber articles can serve the domestic market of northeast, northwest, and central Bangladesh, and selected products can be exported to the northeast Indian market.

(xii) **Electrical and electronics.** Bangladesh is highly dependent on electrical and electronics imports. The imports in the electrical and electronics segment were $4 billion in 2019. Bangladesh has a limited presence in the plastics and rubber industry. Development of these industries is essential, as they form the backward linkage for the electrical and electronics industry. In the short term, Bangladesh can participate actively at the assembly stage of the electrical and electronics industry which, in the future, has the potential to attract foreign direct investment (FDI). With the completion of Electronics City at Sylhet and growing traction at Sheikh Hasina Software Technology Park at Jessore, the Sylhet–Habiganj and Khulna–Jessore nodes can leverage their ecosystem to further consolidate the industry in the region.

(xiii) **Heavy machinery.** Bangladesh is highly dependent on imports for heavy machineries ($7 billion in 2019). The magnitude of the import number shows the existing opportunity in the domestic market. Heavy machineries produced in the domestic market do not have a strong brand to fight imports. The same is observed in the case of spare parts which face significant competition from the spare parts imported from People's Republic of China. Development of new agriprocessing, food processing, textiles and RMGs, leather and leather articles, footwear, furniture, pharmaceuticals, plastic products, and rubber and rubber articles factories in the corridor region is expected to generate demand for new machineries and spare parts in the future. This gives opportunities for the development of this industry in the region.

Along with the manufacturing sector, it is also imperative to assess service sector potential in the corridor region. The service sector is a major industry globally, with a 65% contribution to the overall global GDP; in the case of Bangladesh, it contributes 52% of GDP. Also, many industries under the service sector have high employment intensity, which can help in the holistic development of the economic corridor region. Two major service sector industries, i.e., information technology and tourism are considered for assessment.

(i) **Information technology industry.** Bangladesh's information technology industry is rapidly growing, with exports growing 15.3% year-on-year over the last 10 years compared to the global level (10.9%). Export of telecommunication service is the highest in Bangladesh, followed by computer services and information services. The Government of Bangladesh is developing the required infrastructure for the information technology industry in the country through construction of various hubs and hi-tech parks. There are five major projects coming in the northeast part of the country: Bangabandhu Hi-Tech Park in Gazipur district, Sylhet Electronics City, Mymensingh Information Technology Park, Bangabandhu Hi-Tech City in Khulna, and Sylhet Information Technology Park. These developments are expected to promote the software, information technology, and related hardware industry in the BEC region.

(ii) **Travel and tourism industry.** Travel and tourism contribute 2.2% to the national GDP of Bangladesh. It is expected to increase to 6.2% and to generate 4.2 million jobs by 2028. Northeast Bangladesh hosts several tourist spots in the form of hill stations, waterfalls, and tea gardens. The unique location of the Sylhet district close to the Himalayan ranges presents the potential to be developed into attractive tourist destinations. Tea gardens in the district of Sylhet can also offer amazing landscapes, which can be developed into an attraction for domestic as well as international tourists. Similarly, the Khulna division has mangrove forests and Sundarban has the country's majestic wildlife sanctuary. Also, the region has potential for cruise tourism. However, to bolster the travel and tourism industry, Bangladesh needs to improve transportation and social infrastructure in both NEBEC and SWBEC.

Based on the detailed value chain assessment, industries are identified that will be relatively easier to promote in the corridor region given its inherent advantages and disadvantages. Accordingly, the favorability of these industries in the BEC region is analyzed based on parameters such as domestic market size, technical competency, adequacy of existing infrastructure, domestic availability of input materials, and access to export opportunities. Based on the outcome of the analysis, "Degree of Favorability" of the selected industries is determined (Figure 4).

Figure 4: **Prioritization of Industries Based on their Ease of Promotion in the Corridor Region**

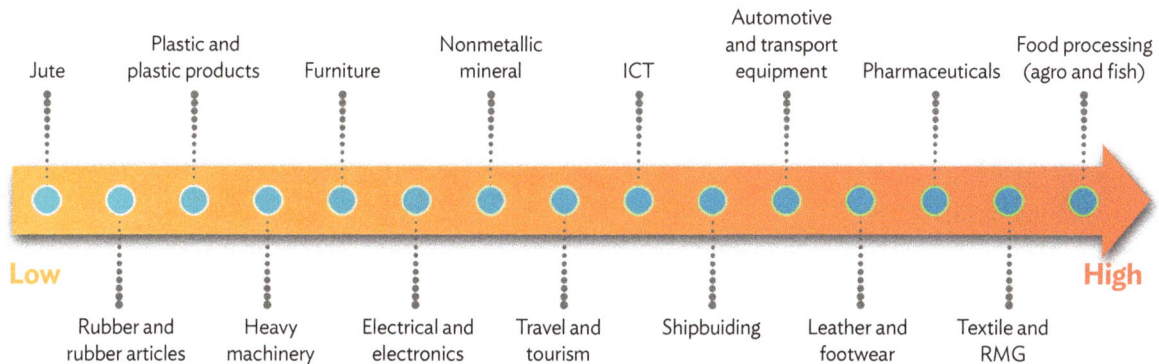

Jute | Plastic and plastic products | Furniture | Nonmetallic mineral | ICT | Automotive and transport equipment | Pharmaceuticals | Food processing (agro and fish)

Low | High

Rubber and rubber articles | Heavy machinery | Electrical and electronics | Travel and tourism | Shipbuiding | Leather and footwear | Textile and RMG

ICT = information and communication technology, RMG = ready-made garments.
Source: Asian Development Bank study team.

Among all the selected industries across the manufacturing and service sectors, suitable industries are mapped for the nodes to assess which localities are more compatible to host them based on parameters like availability of factor of production of that particular industry (access to resources for inputs, availability of water, availability of gas, availability of labor as per skill requirement, and others), access to markets, and other considerations such as pollution levels and existing industrial ecosystem. Based on outcome of the analysis, industries are mapped against respective nodes of BEC (Map 7).

Along with industrial development in these four identified nodes, the Sunamganj cluster can also be developed as the supplier of key input materials for fishing and food and the agro industry. Being a *haor* area, the cluster is one of the largest producers of fish in Bangladesh. The largest domestic consumer market, Dhaka City, and other nodes are well connected with the Sunamganj cluster. Also, the cluster can tap in fish and fish product demand of Northeast India, which can be easily accessed via the Tamabil and Nakugaon land ports.

Map 7: Key Industries Mapped against Nodes of Bangladesh Economic Corridor

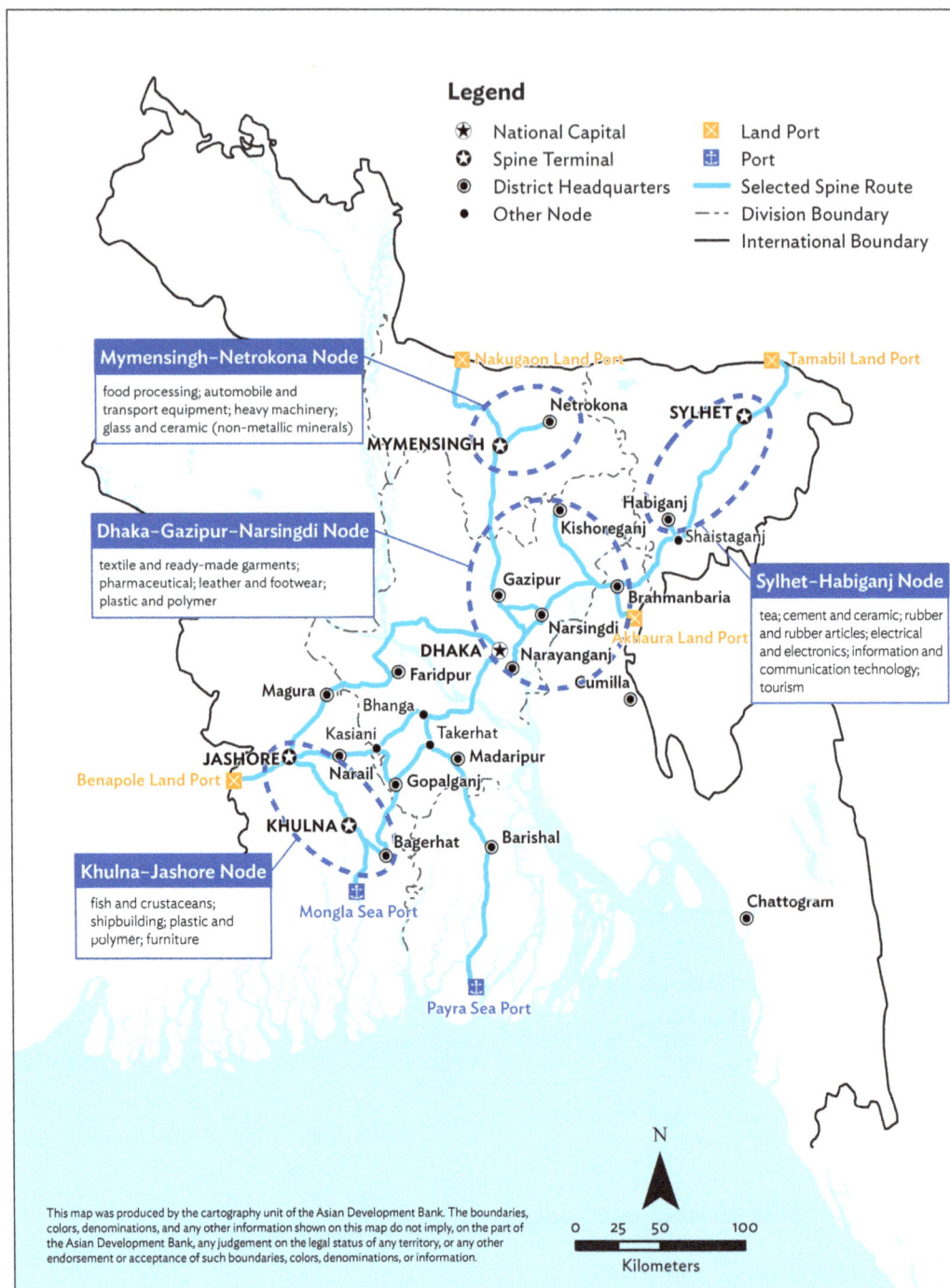

Legend

- ✪ National Capital
- ✪ Spine Terminal
- ◉ District Headquarters
- ● Other Node
- ▣ Land Port
- ⊞ Port
- ▬ Selected Spine Route
- --- Division Boundary
- — International Boundary

Mymensingh–Netrokona Node

food processing; automobile and transport equipment; heavy machinery; glass and ceramic (non-metallic minerals)

Dhaka–Gazipur–Narsingdi Node

textile and ready-made garments; pharmaceutical; leather and footwear; plastic and polymer

Sylhet–Habiganj Node

tea; cement and ceramic; rubber and rubber articles; electrical and electronics; information and communication technology; tourism

Khulna–Jashore Node

fish and crustaceans; shipbuilding; plastic and polymer; furniture

Nakugaon Land Port   Tamabil Land Port

Netrokona   SYLHET

MYMENSINGH

Habiganj
Kishoreganj   Shaistaganj

Gazipur   Brahmanbaria

Narsingdi   Akhaura Land Port

DHAKA
Faridpur   Narayanganj

Magura   Cumilla
Bhanga
Kasiani   Takerhat
JASHORE   Narail   Madaripur
Benapole Land Port   Gopalganj

KHULNA   Barishal
Bagerhat

Chattogram

Mongla Sea Port

Payra Sea Port

N

This map was produced by the cartography unit of the Asian Development Bank. The boundaries, colors, denominations, and any other information shown on this map do not imply, on the part of the Asian Development Bank, any judgement on the legal status of any territory, or any other endorsement or acceptance of such boundaries, colors, denominations, or information.

0   25   50   100

Kilometers

Source: Asian Development Bank study team.

Transport Corridor and Trade Gateways

As explained earlier, production clusters are the main drivers of economic growth in the corridor, but they must be supported by an efficient and effective transport infrastructure. Transport linkages are essential for connectivity within the corridor region, to key hinterlands outside the corridor region, and to trade gateways. An efficient transport infrastructure acts as a catalyst of economic growth by enabling seamless movement of passenger and freight. An effective transport network requires integrated planning and development of multimodal means of transport and logistic infrastructure.

Multimodal trunk transport connectivity comprises roadways, railways, and inland and coastal waterways with adequate feeder networks, connecting industrial and urban agglomerations, and trade gateways. Therefore, it is important to identify and prioritize projects across various modes of transportation. For assessment of capacity augmentation for each transport mode, traffic was projected. For that, first, existing traffic volume and traffic flow (origin-destination movement) in respective transport modes was analyzed. Furthermore, the traffic volume was projected based on freight traffic growth and passenger traffic growth. Freight traffic growth was projected based on industrial output estimation in the region, and passenger traffic growth was projected based on GDP per capita. Based on future traffic volume (freight and passenger together), capacity augmentation for each transport mode has been planned. Furthermore, transport mode-wise specific projects have been identified and prioritized (Figure 5).

Figure 5: **Framework for Assessment of Transport Augmentation Plan for Different Transport Modes**

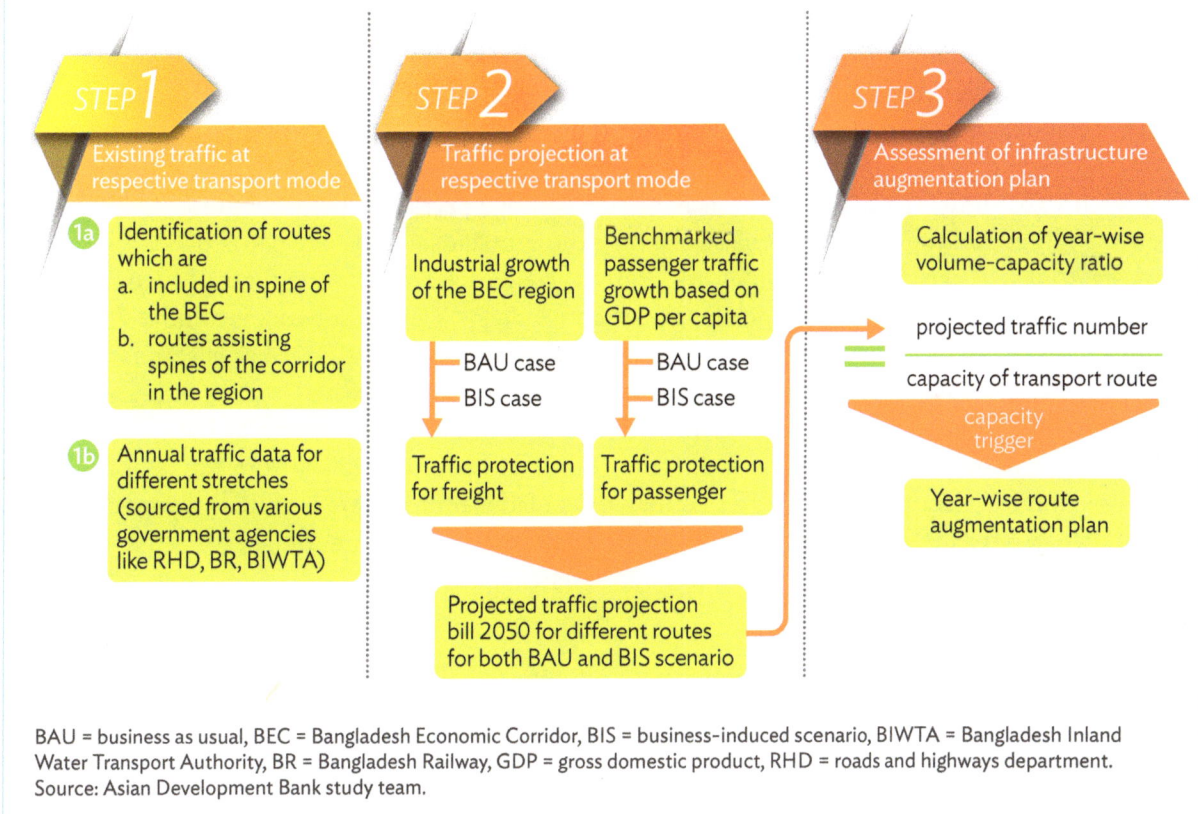

BAU = business as usual, BEC = Bangladesh Economic Corridor, BIS = business-induced scenario, BIWTA = Bangladesh Inland Water Transport Authority, BR = Bangladesh Railway, GDP = gross domestic product, RHD = roads and highways department.
Source: Asian Development Bank study team.

Strengthening the Transportation Network

Key terminals of the economic corridor region, i.e., Dhaka, Mymensingh, Sylhet, Jessore, and Khulna, are connected by four major highways: Dhaka–Mymensingh (N3), Dhaka–Sylhet (N2), Dhaka–Jessore (N7), and Dhaka–Khulna (N805). Road connectivity in N7 and N805 involve ferry crossings, e.g., Paturia. The state of infrastructure at these ferry crossings is inadequate.

Challenges include congested approach roads, inadequate parking facilities, and a limited number of ferries in operation. It has been observed that generally, more than 4 hours is typically spent at the Paturia River crossing. However, with the opening of the Padma Bridge in 2022, an alternative to ferry crossing has been available and significantly reduced travel time. Still, many road stretches in these four major highways and other roads and highways in the corridor region suffer from overcapacity. In addition, the presence of a *haor* area in Sunamganj, Netrokona, and Habiganj districts restricts infrastructure development in the northeast economic corridor (Map 8).

With the rising development in the region, the demand for capacities of the key routes in the spine is likely to rise. Furthermore, with due consideration of the spine(s) and the location of the nodes, urban agglomeration, and trade gateways and key stretches, the BEC recommends 114 unique road connectivity projects covering 5,000 km.

Major road stretches in BEC where lane augmentation is required are N7: Paturia River Crossing to Mongla (254 km); N8: Dhaka to Patuakhali (205 km); N805: Bhanga to Katakhali via Gopalganj (117 km); N702: Magura to Jessore (43 km); Mogorkhal to Mymensingh (110 km); Mogorkhal to Mirer Bazar (10 km); Mirerbazar to Bhulta (23 km); Bhulta to Ashuganj (62 km); Sylhet–Tamabil Road (52 km); Biswa Road Bus Station to Bara Sultanpur on Comilla Highway (20 km); Sherpur–Mymensingh Highway (48 km), and others.

Completion of these identified projects will improve road connectivity in the corridor region and will improve the volume–capacity ratio, easing traffic congestion in major road stretches.

Along with road network development, it is critical to develop railways, which are cheaper, for an effective multimodal transport network. Currently, the Bangladesh rail network is divided into East and West zones. Three different gauges are present in the railway network: meter gauge, standard gauge, and broad gauge. The total track length of Bangladesh's railway network is around 2,900 km, around 1,800 km of which is meter gauge, 660 km is broad gauge, and 409 km is standard gauge. Bangladesh has mostly meter gauge on the eastern side of the Jamuna River and broad gauge on the western side. Differences in gauge standards in the western and eastern parts of Bangladesh deter efficient movement of freight wagons within the country. In addition, apart from Komolapur Inland Container Depot (ICD) in Dhaka (and a planned ICD at Dhirsaram), there is no ICD planned in other parts of the country, including the corridor region, which hinders container freight movement via rail.

Map 8: Challenges along Bangladesh Economic Corridor Transportation Routes

Legend

★ National Capital
✪ Spine Terminal
◉ District Headquarters
• Other Node
⬡ haor

⊠ Land Port
⊞ Port
── Selected Spine Route
--- Division Boundary
── International Boundary

Large *haor* region restricts direct road connectivity between Mymensingh and Sylhet

Nakugaon Land Port
Tamabil Land Port

Netrokona
MYMENSINGH
SYLHET

Habiganj
Kishoreganj
Shaistaganj

Gazipur
Brahmanbaria

Paturia River Crossing

Narsingdi
Akhaura Land Port

DHAKA
Narayanganj
Faridpur
Cumilla

Magura
Bhanga
Kasiani
Takerhat
Narail
Madaripur
JASHORE
Gopalganj
Benapole Land Port

KHULNA
Bagerhat
Barishal

Mongla Sea Port

Chattogram

Payra Sea Port

N

0 25 50   100
Kilometers

This map was produced by the cartography unit of the Asian Development Bank. The boundaries, colors, denominations, and any other information shown on this map do not imply, on the part of the Asian Development Bank, any judgement on the legal status of any territory, or any other endorsement or acceptance of such boundaries, colors, denominations, or information.

Note: A *haor* area is a flood-prone shallow land.
Source: Asian Development Bank study team.

Hence, to improve rail share in the entire corridor region, 62 projects have been identified, 34 of which pertain to gauge standardization (meter gauge, dual gauge, broad gauge) in key routes like Laksam to Akhaura, Akhaura to Sylhet, Sylhet to Chatak Bazaar, Gouripur Junction to Mohanganj, Bhairab Bazar to Gauripur Junction. Standardization will not only address gauge compatibility within Bangladesh, but also enable efficient rail movement with India. In addition, 17 projects related to new route development or route upgradation have been identified in key routes like Jessore to Bhanga to Dhaka (via Padma bridge), Khulna to Bagerhat, Jessore to Darsana land port, and others.

Furthermore, four projects related to rail route electrification have been identified: Tongi to Chattogram (via Akhaura), Akhaura to Sylhet, Dhaka to Mymensingh (via Joydebpur), and Mymensingh to Bhairab Bazaar; these will help to address wagon compatibility and bring down operational costs. Also, seven new ICD development projects—Khulna, Bagerhat, Dhaka cluster, Jessore, Dhirasram, Mymensingh and Shaitaganj—have been identified that will improve container traffic movement via railways.

Along with rail and road network development, it is critical to develop the IWT network for the corridor region as it provides natural connectivity with the Indian states of Assam, Meghalaya, and West Bengal. However, low natural draft along with irregular dredging have restrained capacity of movement of barges beyond Dhaka. Navigational issues have constrained the corridor region from tapping into any cross-border trade potential through the Dhulian–Rajshahi–Aricha, Ashuganj–Zakiganj, and Ashuganj–Dawki Indo–Bangladesh Protocol route stretch.

For development of IWT infrastructure in the corridor region, 30 projects have been identified for navigation channels and augmenting infrastructure at river ports and/or inland container terminals (Map 9).

The following navigation channels are proposed:

(i) The Dhaka–Chandpur–Madaripur–Gopalganj–Khulna route, currently a Class 2 route, may be developed into Class 1 route. This route is closer to the spines of the corridor compared to the former, and provide a shorter inland waterways connectivity between Dhaka and Khulna (330 km), compared to the other inland waterway routes, i.e., Dhaka–Chanpur–Barisal–Hularhut–Khulna (437 km).

(ii) The Ashuganj–Ghoradigha–Gaglajor–Durlavpur route, currently a Class 2 route, needs to be developed into a Class 1 route. Furthermore, the Durlavpur–Takerghat stretch, currently a Class 3 route, should be developed into a Class 1 route. Hence, the entire stretch from Dhaka–Ashuganj–Takerghat will be a Class 1 route.

(iii) Also, Ashuganj to Sherpur–Zakiganj, currently a Class 3 route, may be also developed as a Class 1 route considering its strategic proximity to the resource-rich Indian states of Assam and Meghalaya.[8]

---

[8] Class I waterway has a draft of 3.66–3.96 meters (m); Class II waterway has a draft of 1.83–3.65 m; Class III waterway has a draft of 0.91–1.82 m and Class IV waterway has a draft of less than 0.91 m.

Map 9: **Inland Waterway Transport Infrastructure Development along Bangladesh Economic Corridor**

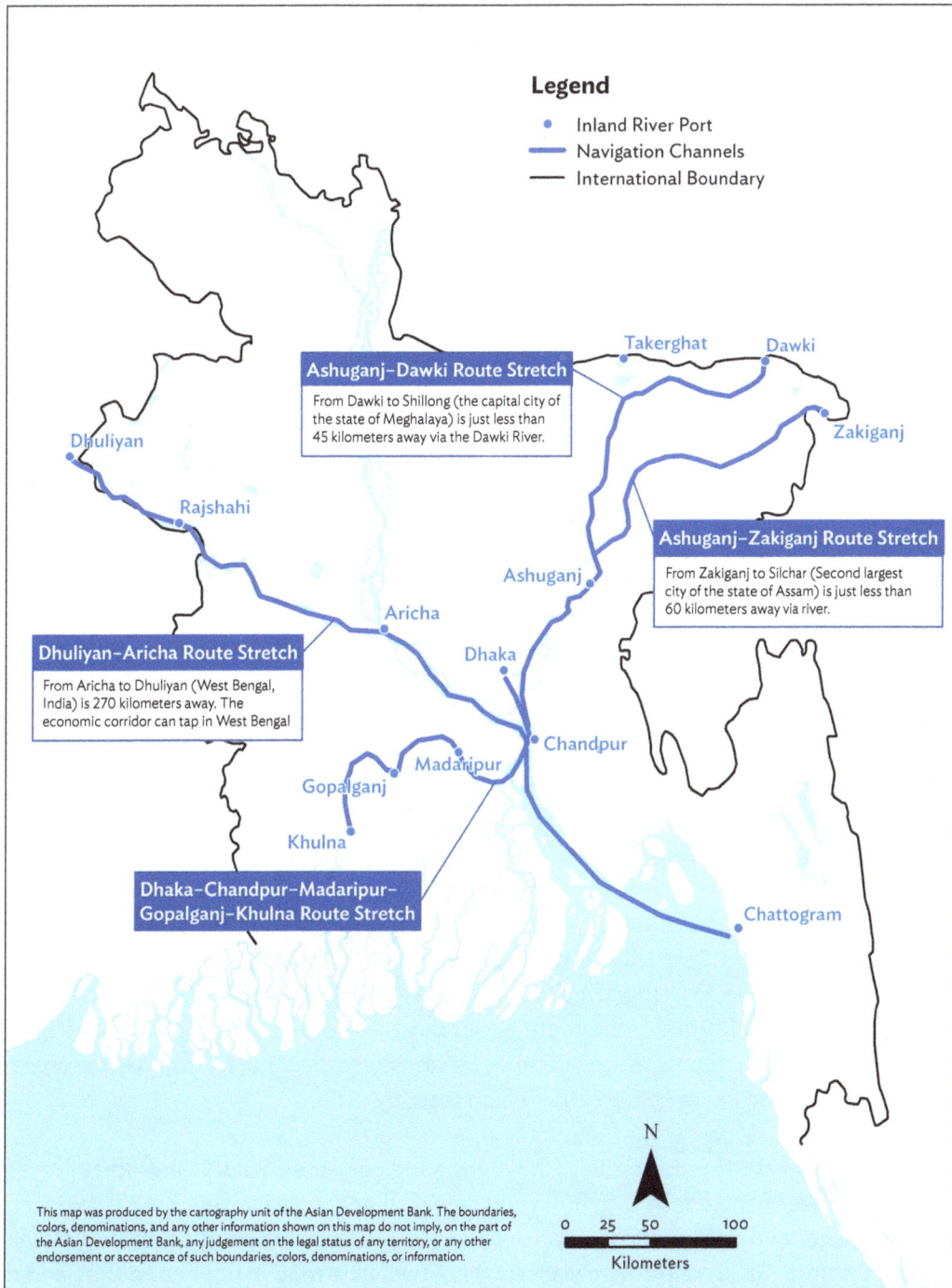

Legend

- Inland River Port
- Navigation Channels
- International Boundary

Ashuganj–Dawki Route Stretch

From Dawki to Shillong (the capital city of the state of Meghalaya) is just less than 45 kilometers away via the Dawki River.

Ashuganj–Zakiganj Route Stretch

From Zakiganj to Silchar (Second largest city of the state of Assam) is just less than 60 kilometers away via river.

Dhuliyan–Aricha Route Stretch

From Aricha to Dhuliyan (West Bengal, India) is 270 kilometers away. The economic corridor can tap in West Bengal

Dhaka–Chandpur–Madaripur–Gopalganj–Khulna Route Stretch

Takerghat · Dawki · Zakiganj · Dhuliyan · Rajshahi · Ashuganj · Aricha · Dhaka · Chandpur · Madaripur · Gopalganj · Khulna · Chattogram

This map was produced by the cartography unit of the Asian Development Bank. The boundaries, colors, denominations, and any other information shown on this map do not imply, on the part of the Asian Development Bank, any judgement on the legal status of any territory, or any other endorsement or acceptance of such boundaries, colors, denominations, or information.

N

0   25   50   100

Kilometers

Source: Asian Development Bank study team.

For developing efficient river terminals, infrastructure at the Ashuganj and Chattak river ports can be augmented, given that two river ports are strategically located to serve the urban centers near the Sylhet–Habibganj node. Furthermore, infrastructure at Narayanganj, Narsingdi, Aricha, and Tongi (Gazipur) may be strategically developed over time to effectively cater to the production centers in the Dhaka node. Another new river port facility may be planned at Zakiganj to effectively cater to international trade cargo on this Indo–Bangladesh Protocol route.

Execution of all these identified projects will promote inland waterways for freight and passenger transport beyond Dhaka.

Along with road, rail, and IWT, infrastructure of trade gateways of the corridor region also faces capacity constraints. The only functional port in the corridor region, Mongla Port, is currently underutilized, with low ship call frequency and a draft of around 7–8 meter. The port currently handles only about 9% of the seaborne traffic of Bangladesh (11 million metric tons in 2019). There are several reasons behind Mongla Port's underutilization. The infrastructure and equipment available at Mongla Port was procured more than 35 years ago and has completed its effective life. Moreover, the connectivity between Mongla Port and the hinterland is largely inadequate. The last-mile road to Mongla Port is two-lane, and, at present, there is no railway linkage to the port. Thus, there is a need for new seaports and upgrading of existing ones. A new seaport project is under construction at Payra in Patuakhali District of southern Bangladesh.

The traffic generated by the envisaged corridor will comprise goods produced therein for exports, and imports of inputs (intermediates and raw materials) for the goods that will be produced therein. The imports in the beginning are likely to consist of intermediates, but with the long-term development of backward linkages, the imports will gradually be more of raw materials. Imports of inputs is likely to continue in the future, as Bangladesh is a natural resource-deficient country.

It has been estimated that the seaports in Bangladesh, including the upcoming ports, may have to cater to total traffic of 194 million tons by 2030 and 536 million tons by 2050. The distribution of traffic from the hinterland to these ports will depend on overall logistics cost savings. It has been estimated that Payra Port and Mongla Port will be more economical for the districts to the west of Padma River, while the ports in the Chattogram division (the existing Chattogram Port and the upcoming ports and/or terminals) will prove to be more economical for the southern districts of Bangladesh. Considering that, the comprehensive development plan suggests capacity augmentation of Mongla Port to 65 million tons and Payra Port to 265 million tons, by 2050.

Land ports are critical gateways for trade with neighboring countries. All six land ports present in the corridor region connect Bangladesh with India and face challenges with respect to the lack of last-mile connectivity, storage, and cargo infrastructure. For example, the offtake road to and from Bhomra Land port (i.e., Bhomra–Satkhira–Khulna via R760) is a two-lane road in poor condition, and there are constraints in last-mile connectivity from Sherpur–Nakugaon stretch (R371) for Nakugaon land port and Sujanagar to Bibirbazaar land port (10 km).

In addition, Benapole land port, one of the largest between India and Bangladesh, faces acute shortage of storage capacity. Current storage capacity at Benapole of 40,000 metric tons is insufficient compared to an estimated requirement of 100,000–150,000 metric tons generated by 200–250 trucks arriving daily with goods to be exported to India and 400–450 trucks arriving with imported goods from India. This leads to a backlog at both sides of the border, causing heavy traffic congestion. The backlog at Benapole causes an average delay of 5–6 days. To counter this delay, transporters charge higher rates, making the trading process more expensive. Furthermore, none of the land ports in the corridor region have proper container facilities.

To address these challenges, 28 projects have been identified. While completion of the Sylhet–Tamabil four-lane expansion project (Asian Infrastructure Investment Bank-funded) and Akhaura–Ashuganj four-lane expansion (as part of the Indo–Bangladesh Bilateral Agreement) road project will fill the immediate gap in terms of last-mile connectivity, three more projects have been identified for last-mile connectivity of Bibirbazar, Bhomra, and Nakugaon land ports. Going forward, two land ports, i.e., Benapole and Bhomra, will face capacity constraints. For that, capacity at both Benapole and Bhomra land port needs to be increased to 12 million tons by 2030 and 20 million tons by 2050. Also, lack of coordination among various trade agencies poses a significant challenge. Hence, automation of business processes at all land ports needs to be expedited, along with implementation of a common software platform for all trade agencies.

There are four operational airports in Bangladesh: Dhaka, Jessore, Barishal, and Sylhet in the corridor region. In the short term, Dhaka Airport will continue to operate under full capacity (current passenger traffic of 9.7 million against designated capacity of 8 million) until the opening of the third terminal in 2023 (expected). With its timely completion (cumulative capacity is expected to reach 20 million) and the commencement of Bangabandhu Sheikh Mujib International Airport, sufficient capacity will exist for the medium to long term to cater to the expected base demand of the Dhaka catchment area.

The Sylhet Airport is currently operating at 98% utilization level (air passenger traffic of 0.59 million against designated capacity of 0.6 million). With the completion of existing expansion work, Sylhet Airport's cumulative capacity is expected to reach 2 million. Thus, capacity augmentation plans need to be in sync with passenger traffic growth. In 2050, passenger traffic at Sylhet Airport is expected to reach 10.6 million. Furthermore, commencement of two greenfield airports at Payra (Patuakhali Airport) and Khulna (Bagerhat Airport) will create additional capacity in the corridor catchment area.

Due to of the foregoing, strategy should be focused on service upgrades and operational de-bottlenecking like enhancing warehousing infrastructure, augmenting cargo equipment, improving customs, and others. Completion of road, rail, inland water, and air transport connectivity will ensure efficient multimodal connectivity in the BEC region (Map 10).

Map 10: Completion of Transport Projects Will Ensure Efficient Multimodal Transport Connectivity in Bangladesh Economic Corridor Region

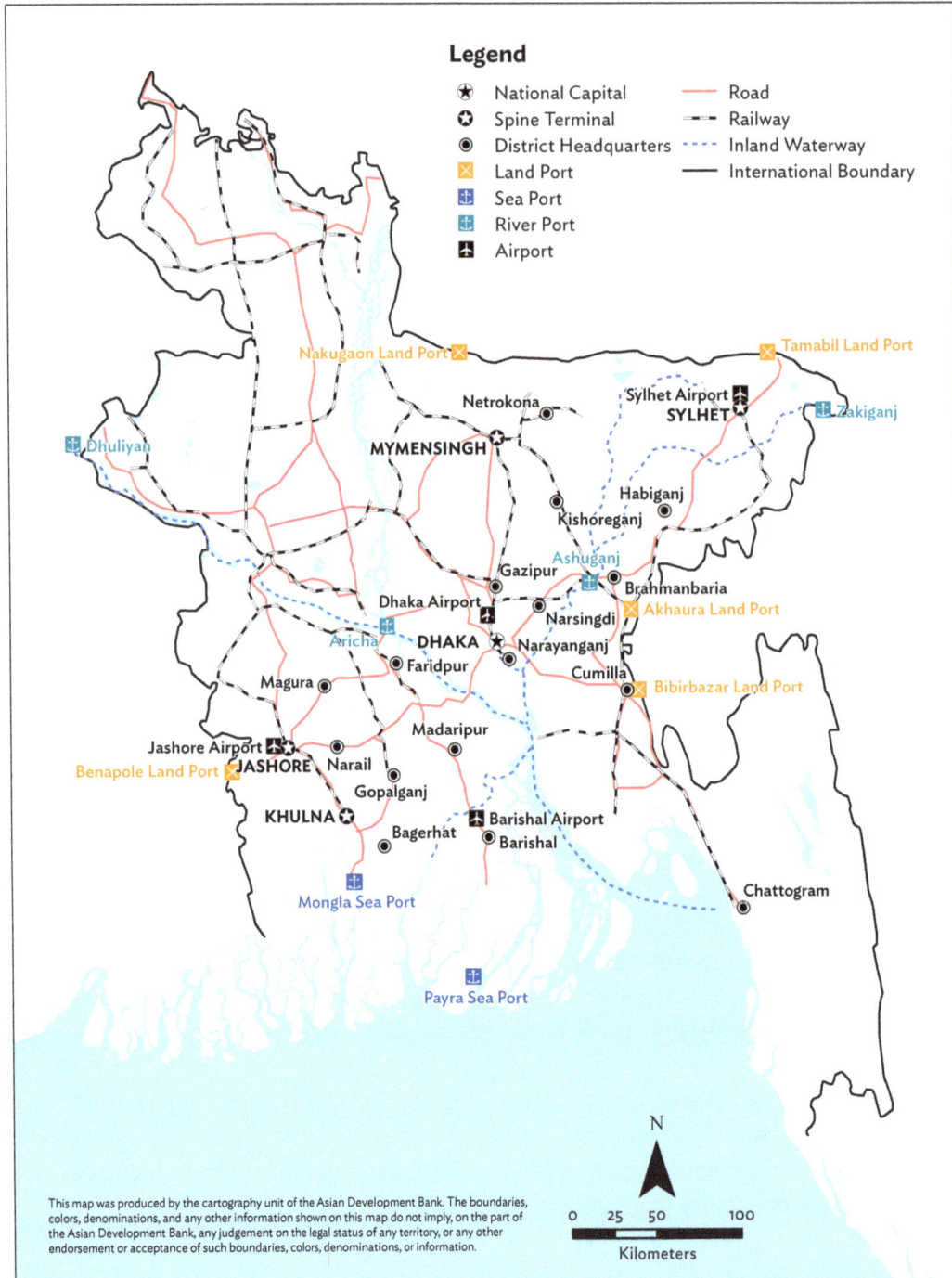

Legend

- ★ National Capital
- ✪ Spine Terminal
- ◉ District Headquarters
- ▨ Land Port
- ⚓ Sea Port
- ⚓ River Port
- ✈ Airport
- — Road
- –·– Railway
- –·– Inland Waterway
- — International Boundary

Nakugaon Land Port
Tamabil Land Port
Netrokona
Sylhet Airport
SYLHET
Zakiganj
Dhuliyan
MYMENSINGH
Habiganj
Kishoreganj
Ashuganj
Gazipur
Brahmanbaria
Dhaka Airport
Narsingdi
Akhaura Land Port
Aricha
DHAKA
Narayanganj
Faridpur
Cumilla
Magura
Bibirbazar Land Port
Madaripur
Jashore Airport
JASHORE   Narail
Benapole Land Port
Gopalganj
KHULNA
Barishal Airport
Bagerhat   Barishal
Mongla Sea Port
Chattogram
Payra Sea Port

N

0   25   50   100
Kilometers

This map was produced by the cartography unit of the Asian Development Bank. The boundaries, colors, denominations, and any other information shown on this map do not imply, on the part of the Asian Development Bank, any judgement on the legal status of any territory, or any other endorsement or acceptance of such boundaries, colors, denominations, or information.

Source: Asian Development Bank study team.

Power Sector Strategy

The power sector is the backbone of the corridor's industrial and infrastructural development as it drives construction, industrial, and economic activities. An effective power sector plan requires integrated development of the major constituents of the power sector value chain, namely, generation, transmission, and distribution. To buttress the power generation capacity with cleaner energy, the government should directly focus on development of renewables-based generation. On this premise, the priority projects for supporting development of BEC shall include the completion of renewables projects in Power System Master Plan 2016 by 2025 (Figure 6).

Figure 6: Capacity Addition on Account of Bangladesh Economic Corridor Region Demand
(megawatts)

	2025–2030	2030–2035	2035–2040	2040–2050
Addn. (Industralization and Infrastructure)	969	1,173	2,790	13,035
Addn. (Urbanization Share)	1,239	1,501	3,566	16,661
BAU Scenario	6,493	4,031	6,716	19,201

BAU = business as usual.
Source: Asian Development Bank study team.

About 90.8 gigawatts (GW) total capacity addition will be required in the Bangladesh generation ecosystem to adequately address the demand under business as usual (BAU) as it pertains to the BEC region. The BEC region would require 50 GW to meet the demand under BAU. Furthermore, the remaining 41 GW would be required to support the additional BEC related demand, with 22.9 GW to meet the urbanization needs and 18 GW for industrialization and infrastructure development requirements. Considering the development in and around the identified nodes in the BEC region, the augmentation and development of transmission and distribution infrastructure is going to be a critical activity. Hence, there shall be an urgent requirement of strengthening transmission and distribution networks in the region to cater to the existing as well as envisaged additional load generated from the corridor development (Figure 7).

Figure 7: Additional Substation Capacity Addition
(megavolt-amperes)

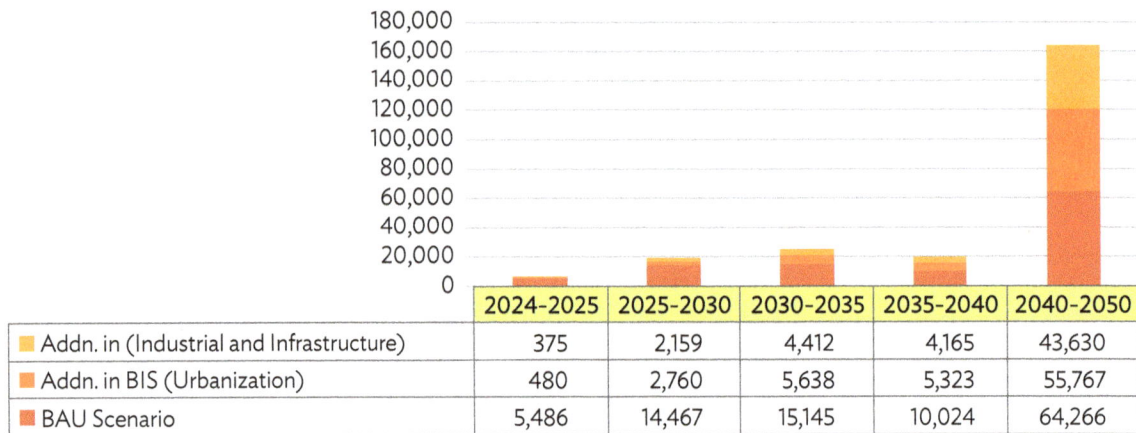

	2024-2025	2025-2030	2030-2035	2035-2040	2040-2050
Addn. in (Industrial and Infrastructure)	375	2,159	4,412	4,165	43,630
Addn. in BIS (Urbanization)	480	2,760	5,638	5,323	55,767
BAU Scenario	5,486	14,467	15,145	10,024	64,266

BAU = business as usual, BIS = business-induced scenario.
Source: Asian Development Bank study team.

On these lines, nearly eight projects have been envisaged for the development of transmission capacity augmentation activity in the BEC region, amounting to an investment of $3.35 billion with additional investment of $6.4 billion aimed toward overall grid strengthening and reliability enhancement of the power system. Post-2025, the BEC region would observe progressive substation capacity and transmission line addition due to the growing demand. Owing to urbanization, the region would require transmission substation capacity of 69,968 megavolt-amperes (MVA) and 54,740 MVA due to industrial and infrastructure developments. Moreover, the transmission circuit length addition of 14,152 circuit kilometers (ckt km) would only meet the BAU demand; there would be need for an additional transmission circuit length installation of 9,680 ckt km (on account of urbanization) and 7,573 ckt km (on account of industrialization and infrastructure) (Figure 8).

In distribution, to renovate and expand the existing distribution infrastructure of the distribution entities in the BEC region, there are certain interventions which will be required to strengthen the last leg of the power sector value chain. Under BAU Scenario, the BEC region would require the circuit capacity addition of 121,300 ckt km, alongside the renovation of 2,829,800 ckt km of distribution lines. Owing to additional demand due to BEC region developments, the line addition of 58,400 ckt km would be required on account of urbanization, and 45,700 ckt km on account of industrialization and infrastructure development (Figure 9).

Figure 8: Additional Transmission Circuit Length Addition
(circuit kilometer)

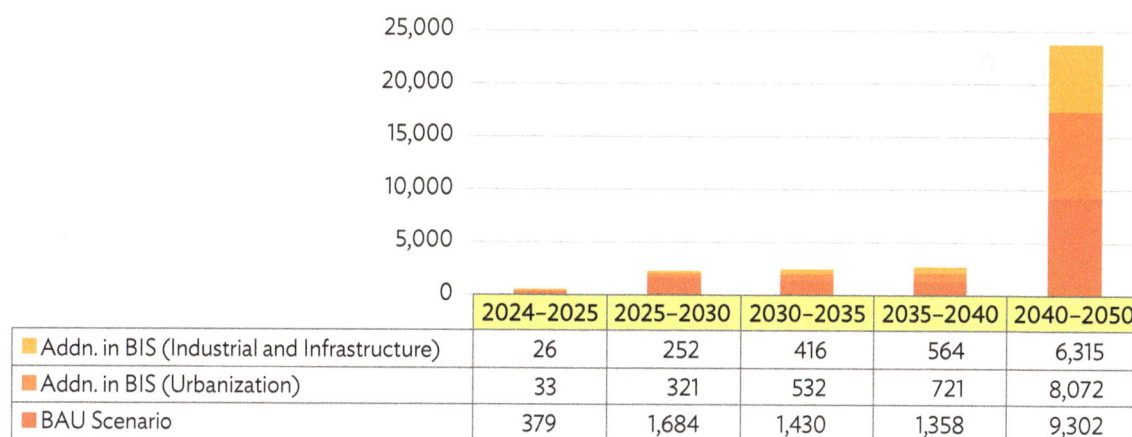

	2024–2025	2025–2030	2030–2035	2035–2040	2040–2050
Addn. in BIS (Industrial and Infrastructure)	26	252	416	564	6,315
Addn. in BIS (Urbanization)	33	321	532	721	8,072
BAU Scenario	379	1,684	1,430	1,358	9,302

BAU = business as usual, BIS = business-induced scenario.
Source: Asian Development Bank study team.

Figure 9: Additional Distribution Line Construction
('000 kilometer)

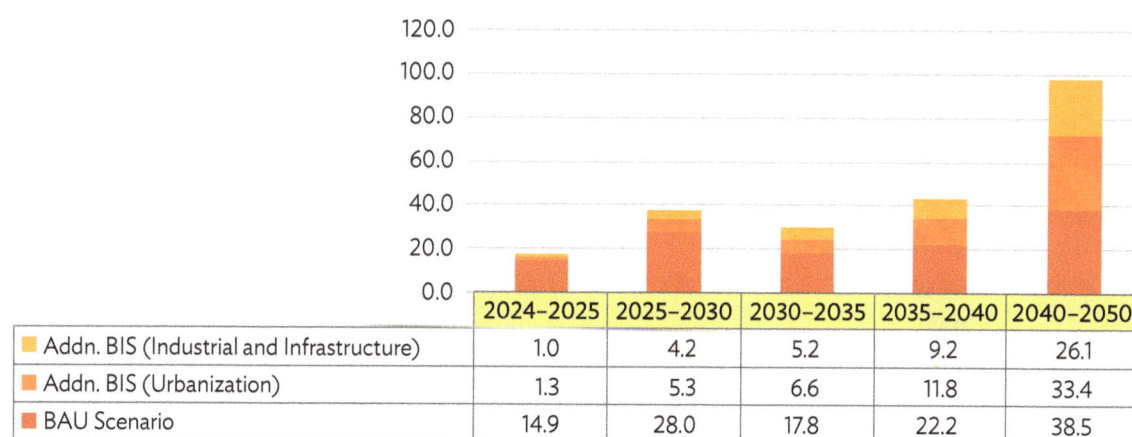

	2024–2025	2025–2030	2030–2035	2035–2040	2040–2050
Addn. BIS (Industrial and Infrastructure)	1.0	4.2	5.2	9.2	26.1
Addn. BIS (Urbanization)	1.3	5.3	6.6	11.8	33.4
BAU Scenario	14.9	28.0	17.8	22.2	38.5

BAU = business as usual, BIS = business-induced scenario.
Source: Asian Development Bank study team.

For substation capacity addition, which is required to strengthen distribution and facilitate last-mile connectivity, the BEC region would require total capacity addition of 44,100 MVA in the 33/11 kilovolts (kV) substation category and 32,820 MVA capacity addition under the 11/0.4 kV substation category. Additional capacity in the 33/11 kV substation segment of 22,300 MVA would be required for urbanization and 17,475 MVA for industrialization and infrastructure. Moreover, in the 11/0.4 kV transformer category, additional capacity addition of 16,490 MVA would be required for urbanization and 12,900 MVA for industrialization and infrastructure developments (Figure 10).

Figure 10: Additional Distribution Substations
(kilovolt)

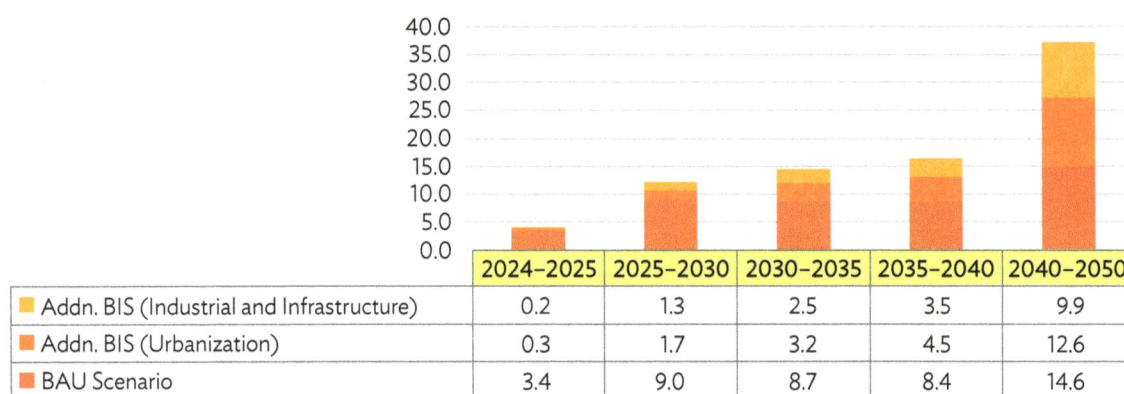

	2024–2025	2025–2030	2030–2035	2035–2040	2040–2050
■ Addn. BIS (Industrial and Infrastructure)	0.2	1.3	2.5	3.5	9.9
■ Addn. BIS (Urbanization)	0.3	1.7	3.2	4.5	12.6
■ BAU Scenario	3.4	9.0	8.7	8.4	14.6

BAU = business as usual, BIS = business-induced scenario.
Source: Asian Development Bank study team.

Moreover, considering the potential growth in the demand trends, Bangladesh is also exploring further power imports from neighboring countries to cater to its growing power needs. There are multiple projects in different phases, which are expected to materialize in the next few years to augment the capacity in Bangladesh and strengthen the enabling grid infrastructure in the nation. Currently, Bangladesh is importing 6.8 billion units from India. Going forward, the cross-border electricity trade is expected to contribute 9,000 MW by 2041, nearly 15% of the envisioned installed capacity.

Along with transportation and power infrastructure, it is important to strengthen social infrastructure to enable holistic and inclusive development. Social infrastructure primarily encompasses education facilities and healthcare facilities. The CDP recommends developing 12,150 education institutions (9,600 secondary schools, 1,950 colleges, 450 technical and vocational institutions, and 130 universities) in the corridor region by 2050 (Map 11). With development of new education institutions, the number of schools per million population is going to increase by 88% to 594 schools per million population in 2050 against 311 schools per million population in 2020. About 50% of educational institutions are going to be developed in the Mymensingh, Dhaka, Sylhet, Jessore, Gazipur, Narayanganj, and Khulna districts.

Map 11: Social Infrastructure Development along Bangladesh Economic Corridor

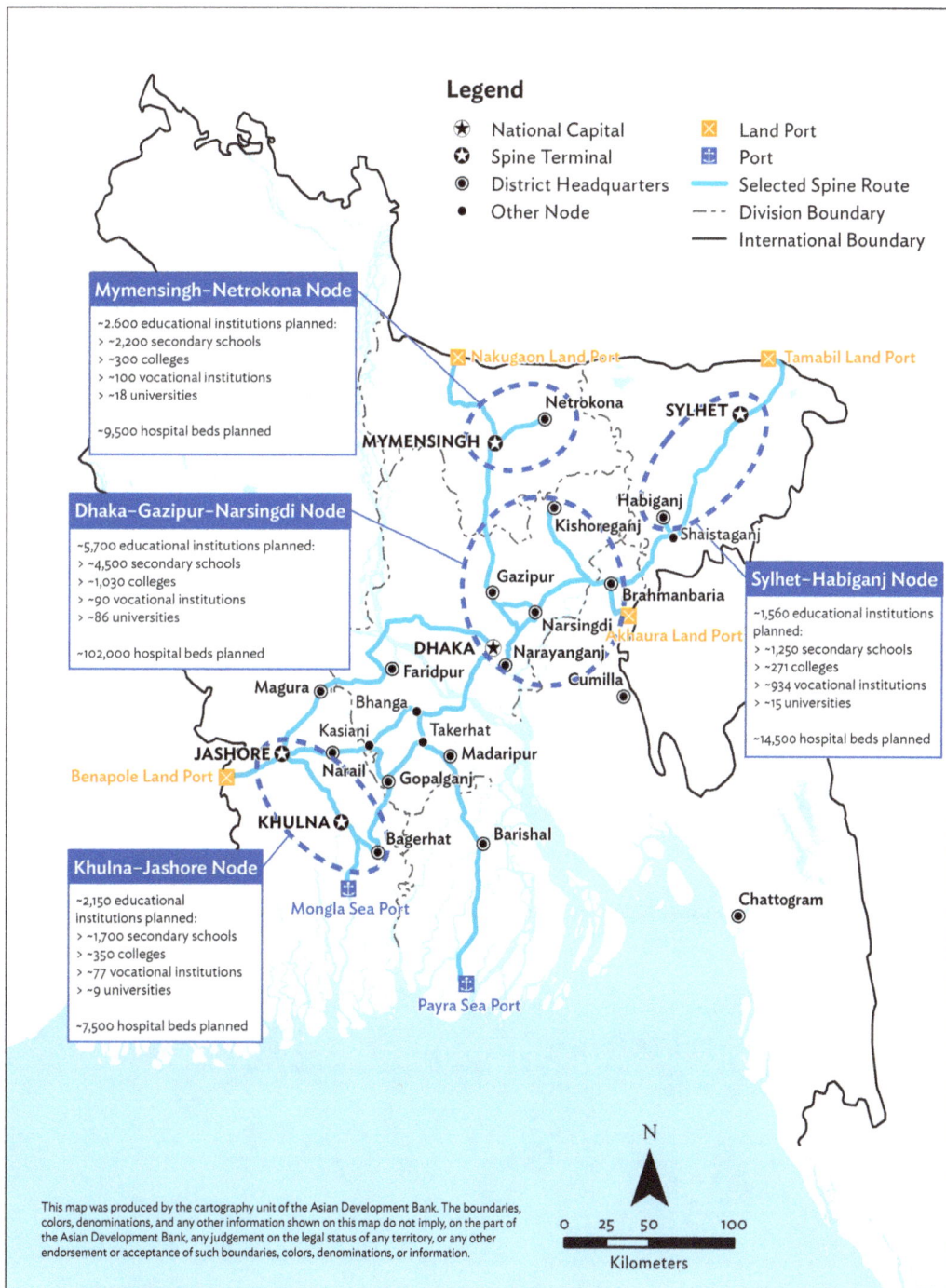

Legend

- ✪ National Capital
- ✪ Spine Terminal
- ◉ District Headquarters
- ● Other Node
- ▨ Land Port
- ✠ Port
- ▬ Selected Spine Route
- – – – Division Boundary
- —— International Boundary

Mymensingh–Netrokona Node

~2,600 educational institutions planned:
- > ~2,200 secondary schools
- > ~300 colleges
- > ~100 vocational institutions
- > ~18 universities

~9,500 hospital beds planned

Dhaka–Gazipur–Narsingdi Node

~5,700 educational institutions planned:
- > ~4,500 secondary schools
- > ~1,030 colleges
- > ~90 vocational institutions
- > ~86 universities

~102,000 hospital beds planned

Sylhet–Habiganj Node

~1,560 educational institutions planned:
- > ~1,250 secondary schools
- > 271 colleges
- > ~934 vocational institutions
- > ~15 universities

~14,500 hospital beds planned

Khulna–Jashore Node

~2,150 educational institutions planned:
- > ~1,700 secondary schools
- > 350 colleges
- > ~77 vocational institutions
- > ~9 universities

~7,500 hospital beds planned

Nakugaon Land Port · Tamabil Land Port · Netrokona · SYLHET · MYMENSINGH · Habiganj · Kishoreganj · Shaistaganj · Gazipur · Brahmanbaria · Narsingdi · Akhaura Land Port · DHAKA · Narayanganj · Faridpur · Cumilla · Magura · Bhanga · Kasiani · Takerhat · JASHORE · Madaripur · Benapole Land Port · Narail · Gopalganj · KHULNA · Bagerhat · Barishal · Mongla Sea Port · Chattogram · Payra Sea Port

N

0   25   50   100

Kilometers

This map was produced by the cartography unit of the Asian Development Bank. The boundaries, colors, denominations, and any other information shown on this map do not imply, on the part of the Asian Development Bank, any judgement on the legal status of any territory, or any other endorsement or acceptance of such boundaries, colors, denominations, or information.

Source: Asian Development Bank study team.

In health care, CDP recommends increasing 134,000 hospital beds in the BEC region by 2050. With the addition of new hospital beds (government and private combined), the number per million population is going to increase to 1,900 in 2050 from 496 in 2020. Most of the hospital beds are expected to be added in the Mymensingh, Dhaka, Sylhet, Jessore, Gazipur, Narayanganj, and Khulna districts.

Estimating the Potential of the Bangladesh Economic Corridor

The BEC aims to enable competitive industries linking GVCs, create jobs, and upgrade infrastructure aligning with future requirements of urban and social agglomerations. Due to the intervention, the total combined output in the entire economic corridor region is expected to increase from $32 billion in 2020 to $286 billion by 2050 in the business-induced scenario (BIS).[9] Along the timeline, the total corridor region BIS output is expected to split off from the BAU scenario's output and gradually increase to become 1.4 times of the total corridor region BAU output by 2030, and 2.6 times by 2050. Figure 11 below depicts the total output in the corridor region in the BAU scenario and under the BIS.

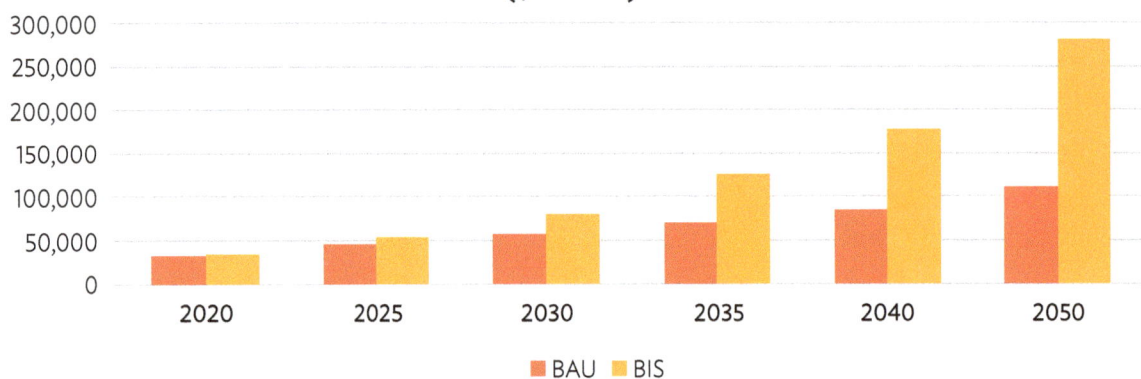

Figure 11: Total Combined Output in the Bangladesh Economic Corridor Region, Business-Induced Scenario versus Business as Usual
($ million)

BAU = business as usual, BIS = business-induced scenario.
Note: Estimated output mentioned is only for a select set of industries. Output numbers are in 2020 prices.
Source: Asian Development Bank study team.

---

[9] The output estimation is carried out in two scenarios: BAU and BIS. In the BAU scenario, a business is expected to run the way it is currently doing, and no special efforts are expected from the public as well as private authority for the promotion of industrial and economic development in the country. On the other hand, in the BIS scenario, the public as well as private players are expected to make special efforts to promote economic development; hence, the industrial growths are estimated higher in the BIS scenario compared to the BAU scenario.

It has been estimated that the whole corridor is expected to generate additional employment of 2.3 million jobs by 2025 and then gradually increase to 40.7 million jobs by 2050. As such, the total employment generated in the corridor region is expected to be 15.7 million in 2025 and 71.8 million in 2050 in the BIS. This is about 2.3 times the employment that is expected to be generated in the corridor region by 2050 compared to the BAU scenario (Figure 12).

Figure 12: Total Combined Employment Generation in Bangladesh Economic Corridor Region
(million)

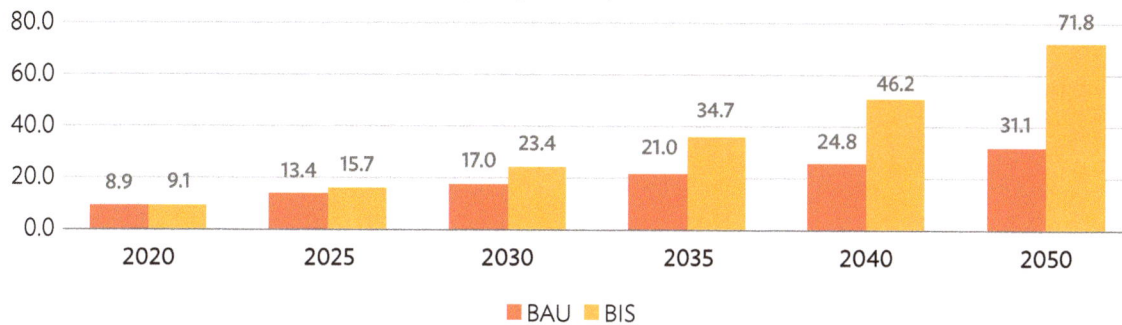

BAU = business as usual, BIS = business-induced scenario.
Note: Estimated output mentioned is only for a select set of industries. Output numbers are in 2020 prices.
Source: Asian Development Bank study team.

In addition to augmenting infrastructure, this study also recommends an effective corridor management mechanism where institutions like BEZA, BEPZA, and BHTPA can be responsible for planning, development, and management of node infrastructure, whereas various line departments will be accountable for planning, development, and management for trunk infrastructure. To ensure coordination between various concerned agencies, the Bangladesh Investment Development Authority (BIDA) will have additional representation from key line ministries like the Ministry of Road Transport and Bridges, the Ministry of Railways, the Ministry of Shipping, and the Ministry of Civil Aviation and Tourism in its Governing Board.

To encourage investment in the BEC region, BIDA, BEZA, BEPZA, and BHTPA could identify target groups of potential investors (both domestic and foreign) against different sectors, business functions, and geographies. Regular interactions with industry associations, trade associations, bilateral chambers of commerce, embassies or high commissions will generate leads for target investors in different sectors. BIDA can organize annual roadshows and business summits that will catalyze government-to-government interactions, government-to-business meetings, and business-to-business engagements. Summits offer an opportunity for attending countries, organizations, and businesses to present their trade and investment proposals to BIDA, BEZA, BEPZA, and/or BHTPA.

An FDI committee with representation from Economic Zone providers (BEZA, BEPZA, BHTPA), BIDA, transport infrastructure providers (Ministry of Roads, Bangladesh Railway, Civil Aviation Authority of Bangladesh, and Bangladesh Inland Water Transport Authority), utility providers, urban infrastructure providers, and the Ministry of Environment can be set up. The committee should be entrusted with evaluation of FDI performance and the review of necessary laws and regulations.

To successfully adopt technology to participate and expand along GVCs, improve the efficiency of industrial processes, and provide support services for the industrial sector in the BEC region, it will be important to focus on human resource development. In addition, there is a need to train the human resource base to adapt to and harness opportunities unleashed by the Fourth Industrial Revolution.